WHAT ARE
ZOOS
FOR?

The status quo is broken. The world is grappling with a web of challenges that could threaten our very existence. If we believe in a better world, now is the time to question the purpose behind our actions and those taken in our name.

Enter the What Is It For? series – a bold exploration of the core elements shaping our world, from religion and free speech to animal rights and the war. This series cuts through the noise to reveal the true impact of these topics, what they really do and why they matter.

Ditching the usual heated debates and polarisations, this series offers fresh, forward-thinking insights. Leading experts present groundbreaking ideas and point to ways forward for real change, urging us to envision a brighter future.

Each book dives into the history and function of its subject, uncovering its role in society and, crucially, how it can be better.

Series editor: George Miller

Visit **bristoluniversitypress.co.uk/what-is-it-for** to find out more about the series.

HEATHER BROWNING is Lecturer in Philosophy at the University of Southampton, working on philosophical questions in animal welfare, sentience and ethics. She previously worked as a zookeeper and zoo animal welfare officer in Australia and New Zealand.

WALTER VEIT is Lecturer in Philosophy at the University of Reading. His primary research interests lie in the intersection of the biological, social and mind sciences and empirically informed philosophy and ethics.

WHAT ARE ZOOS FOR?

HEATHER BROWNING
WALTER VEIT

First published in Great Britain in 2025 by

Bristol University Press
University of Bristol
1–9 Old Park Hill
Bristol
BS2 8BB
UK
t: +44 (0)117 374 6645
e: bup-info@bristol.ac.uk

Details of international sales and distribution partners are available at
bristoluniversitypress.co.uk

British Library Cataloguing in Publication Data
A catalogue record for this book is available from the British Library

ISBN 978-1-5292-3104-5 paperback
ISBN 978-1-5292-3105-2 ePub
ISBN 978-1-5292-3106-9 ePdf

Cover design: Tom Appshaw
Bristol University Press uses environmentally
responsible print partners.
Printed and bound in Great Britain by CPI Group (UK) Ltd,
Croydon, CR0 4YY

FSC
www.fsc.org
MIX
Paper | Supporting
responsible forestry
FSC® C013604

For all the animals living in zoos
– past, present and future

CONTENTS

LIST OF FIGURES AND BOXES

Figures

Boxes

1

INTRODUCTION

What makes for a good zoo? Is it a zoo that provides an entertaining day out? Is it one that treats its animals well, ensuring their health and happiness? Or is it a place that succeeds in educating people about the environment and helps conserve endangered species? There is a divisive ongoing debate about the existence and activities of zoos – about whether and when they are good or bad, and when they are justified. Within this debate are two fundamentally opposed viewpoints: abolition and justification.[1]

Abolitionists say that zoos are unequivocally bad for animals through the very fact of captivity and should therefore be abolished.[2] Zoos, they argue, are places of imprisonment, in which animals live unnatural lives and can never flourish. This entails a strong view about the harm of zoos and a scepticism about the possibility of justifying the existence of zoos. As one employee of an animal protection organization puts it: 'We can't just imprison sentient beings capable of suffering for educational goals while claiming it's pleasurable to see them.'[3] This perspective is typically grounded in the 'rights' position within animal ethics, that emphasizes the fundamental rights that animals possess, such as to life, liberty and humane treatment. On this view, no zoo is a good zoo.

On the other side are the zoo advocates, who see zoos as occupying a unique and important role.[4] They emphasize the range of important activities they see zoos as performing, such as connecting visitors to animals, educating the public about biodiversity and breeding animals for conservation. This, they argue, is sufficient to justify their existence, even if such existence may be regrettable. It's not uncommon to hear zoo staff say that in an ideal world, their job wouldn't need to exist – implying that a world without zoos would be a better one overall, but given the current biodiversity threats they are a necessary evil. In this view, zoos provide sufficiently significant benefits to offset any costs they may impose on their animals. This perspective is typically based in a 'welfare' view in animal ethics, which does not take captivity to be inherently wrong, so long as animals have good lives. In this view, a good zoo is one that provides good welfare for its animals and succeeds at education and conservation aims.

Despite this widespread debate on the ethical status of zoos, they have remained one of the most popular recreational activities, drawing an estimated 700+ million visitors a year.[5] What should one make of this tension? Why is it so challenging to answer the question of whether zoos should exist? It seems that defenders and critics of zoos have fundamentally opposed perspectives that are difficult – if not impossible – to reconcile. It is our aim in this book to address this puzzle, to attempt to find some common ground between the positions and show when and how a zoo can be considered a good zoo. The title of our book asks the question: What are zoos for? And this will be the central question we aim to answer in this book. Only by investigating the goals of zoos can we assess their role in the 21st century and establish what it means to be a good (or bad) zoo.

Our fundamental answer will be a simple but perhaps controversial one: zoos are *for* animals – both the animals in their care, and their counterparts in the wild. While zoos provide benefits to the people who visit them, those who work at them and those in the community who benefit from their activities, these benefits are secondary to those provided for nonhuman animals, instrumental for the larger goals of zoos and are in many cases closely intertwined with those for animals. Importantly, if and when zoos are *not* for animals, they should be. This means that as well as detailing the ways in which we think zoos can and do benefit animals, we will also be highlighting what we see as some of the key changes needed to solidify this role and ensure zoos are truly operating for the good of animals. We will show that zoos are not intrinsically harmful to animals, which means that a well-run zoo need not provide additional reasons, such as the production of scientific knowledge, to justify its existence. The very question of whether zoos can be justified relies on the presumption that they have to offset harms caused to the animals. As we shall argue instead, zoos can be good for animals (indeed, in many cases provide them with better lives than they could have in the wild). Zoos therefore do not need to rationalize their existence; though we will also show how they can successfully perform other roles for the benefit of humans and other animals.

Although we acknowledge that this was not how zoos started, nor how all zoos operate, this doesn't have to mean that it's not how they can be now, or into the future. There are simple reasons in favour of taking the primary function of *good* zoos as benefiting animals. Most of the work hours at a zoo are spent by keepers working to maintain the quality of life of the animals, and the same is true for expenditure (animals are very expensive to house and feed!). Public-facing zoo operations aim to educate, with the ultimate aim of helping wild animals through conservation initiatives. While many might think of zoos as merely existing to satisfy the public desire to watch exotic animals for the sake of profit (see Box 1.1), we will show how they can be so much more.

Misconceptions about zoos are common and Heather has a story of an interaction she experienced when working in a zoo, which illustrates why we decided to write this book.

HB: When I worked in zoos across Australia and New Zealand, one of my favourite parts of the job was

Box 1.1: Walter's perspective

When I was an undergraduate student in philosophy and economics, I viewed zoos through a very economic lens. Thinking of zoos as companies that run based on entry fees, it is easy to conclude that they only exist for the entertainment of their visitors in order to make profit. I think this view is shared by many others – especially critics of zoos – and within such a capitalist framing, it is easy to see why some could even call to abolish them completely. If zoos only exist for human interests, how could the interests of animals possibly be taken seriously? But even if the economics of zoos matter, the conclusion that they only exist for us or for profit would still be a mistake. Zoos today receive funds for a variety of reasons that cannot all be reduced to recreation alone and notably include the interests of the zoo animals themselves. Indeed, 54 per cent of all zoos accredited by the Association of Zoos and Aquariums are non-profit organizations,[6] which should emphasize that the goals of zoos are more complex than a reductive recreation/entertainment picture may suggest. I hope that this book will help to clear up many of the misconceptions people have about zoos, why they are not just for us but also for the animals, and finally to think more deeply about what future zoos should look like.

interacting with the visitors, sharing with them my love of my work and the fantastic animals I got to spend my time with. Whenever I was moving around the park, or in an enclosure cleaning or feeding, I would make time to stop and chat with people nearby, explaining what

I was doing and why, introducing them to whichever animals I happened to be with. One day, I was in an enclosure giving the barking owls Ruby and Rocco their afternoon feed (Figure 1.1). As usual, a couple of people had stopped to watch, and I was telling them about these owls – the two I was working with and the species in general. While the others drifted off after a couple of minutes, one girl stayed behind. I'd just been explaining that these owls – a brother and sister from the same clutch of eggs – had recently turned five, but that this was far from the 20+ years we would expect them to live here.

'But how long would they live if they were in the wild?' she asked me suspiciously.

'Closer to 15 years. They are at risk from competition from introduced species, or predation by bigger owls,' I told her.

'But *most* animals live shorter lives in zoos than in the wild, right?'

I explained to her that while there are some exceptions, most animals actually live longer in captivity – they are protected from disease, predation, food shortages and bad weather. I showed her the food we were feeding them and described some of the ongoing veterinary care and enrichment programmes we provided for the animals.

'Thanks,' she said to me before she left. 'I never liked zoos, but this has changed my mind. I only came today because my family did. I always thought the animals would be suffering, I didn't know all the things you do for them.'

Figure 1.1: Heather with barking owls Ruby and Rocco at the National Zoo and Aquarium

I was pleased to have made such an impact, and the conversation has always stayed with me. It made me realize how many misunderstandings there are among the general public about zoos and the animals they keep; how much outdated information is still commonly believed. I saw how important sharing our work and our stories can be for addressing misconceptions and showing people the reality of life for animals in zoos. It's not perfect, but it's far from the horrors painted by some of the most vehement critics. My experience in zoos shaped my views on the importance of a conversation that takes seriously the worries about captivity while engaging the up-to-date science and practice of zoo husbandry, and this book is the product of this desire.

Part of our goal in this book is not just to answer what zoos are currently for, but also what zoos *should be* for in the future. To do this we will also make reference to the history of zoos to illustrate how much they have changed over the years. But what are zoos anyway? The term 'zoo' originated as an abbreviation of 'zoological garden': an institution housing a collection of different animal species, similar to how botanical gardens showcase the diversity of plant life. Colloquially it typically refers to any institute housing wild animals for public display, including aquariums (Box 1.2). While they are frequently mentioned separately (for example, the World Association of Zoos and Aquariums) the term 'zoo' is often used as a shorthand for both, which is how we will use it here.

Zoos are distinguished from sanctuaries, which hold rehabilitated wild animals unsuitable for release, or animals that have been 'rescued' from places such as zoos, circuses or research institutions, without doing any breeding of their own. Unlike zoos, they are typically large and open range, with no public access. While many zoo abolitionists advocate for housing exotic animals solely in sanctuaries, there is no clean line between the two, and many institutions take advantage of public sympathy for sanctuaries by claiming that is what they are, even when they're not. Many self-proclaimed 'sanctuaries' are merely breeding centres for the wildlife trade, selling animals to unregulated zoos or private collectors. Sanctuaries are important institutions, but ones that serve a very different social role than zoos do, and therefore we will not have space here to include them within the same discussion.

We also want to emphasize here that what we are talking about are the modern 'good' zoos and aquariums. In general, the case against bad zoos is easy. The more interesting and difficult questions are

Box 1.2: Aquariums

Aquariums house aquatic animals – typically fish, sharks and rays, aquatic invertebrates such as crabs and octopus, and marine birds and mammals such as penguins, seals, dolphins, otters and whales. They are broadly similar to zoos in that they are public facilities housing animals for goals such as recreation, education and conservation, but there are some important differences. Aquariums often hold more species, as many types of fish can be kept together in a single tank. There is typically less available knowledge on the housing and husbandry needs of these animals, as well as on how to assess their welfare. Large groups of fish are often managed as a group, with less attention to the individual animals. Unlike in zoos, it is still common for aquariums to collect animals from the wild, which can create both conservation and welfare problems. Some aquatic mammals – such as whales and dolphins – are the subject of high-profile debates around whether they should be held captive at all, due to their intelligence and the fact that their enclosures are usually smaller and more sparsely furnished than those of equivalent land mammals housed in zoos. There has been little discussion so far on the specific ethical challenges of aquariums and this is why in this book we cover them together with zoos.

how we should evaluate modern accredited zoos, and whether they can meet the standards required to be a good zoo whose existence is justified. We want to focus on the current best practice and set out a roadmap for achieving it.

There are, of course, many institutions that fail to meet the standards we are describing, such as the numerous 'roadside zoos' that run entirely for profit, housing animals in small or bare cages (Figure 1.2), without participating in any of the additional activities we will discuss (research, education, conservation). We will not be focusing on these types of institutions, because they are widely condemned, including by the defenders of zoos. Everyone involved in the industry agrees that these are not acceptable, and that they should be made illegal and shut down. Indeed, it is in response to concerns about poor quality zoos that local and international zoo accreditation organizations were formed, such as the World Association of Zoos and Aquariums and the numerous affiliated regional

Figure 1.2: Small, bare cages are typical of a 'roadside' zoo

organizations found throughout the world. These organizations monitor zoos and provide accreditation to those that meet their operating standards. As accredited zoos have been found to be more likely to comply with animal welfare legislation,[7] this provides assurance to visitors and the general public and we recommend that all visitors check online to find out if a zoo is accredited before visiting. By focusing on the best zoos we can assess what is possible with current (and future) best practice and identify the most common areas in need of improvement.

We do not deny that the history of zoos involved plenty of institutions run solely for human benefit. Early zoos emerged from private collections of exotic animals. Over hundreds of years, trade and colonial influence led to many exotic animals being shipped internationally. For instance, rich and powerful members of European society, such as royalty, owned wild and exotic animals both for their own amusement and to display their status, with little regard for animal welfare. At the Tower of London, which once featured animals given to the king of England, is displayed a fragment of a diary from 1786 in which after a visit to the zoo the novelist Sophie von La Roche describes her perception of the boredom, frustration and sorrow of the animals she encountered and laments that 'I was sorry for them, just as it would hurt me to see a fine young man born with good intellect condemned by fate to low, servile, work'.

The long history of holding animals in captivity could easily fill its own book, so we won't even attempt to provide an exhaustive sketch of the origins of zoos (the Further Reading list contains some suggestions for books that provide more detailed zoo histories). Nevertheless, their history is relevant for understanding what zoos have been for, what they are for now and how their future might look. Throughout this book, we will often refer to aspects of zoo history as they relate to the topics we explore. As we hope to make clear, we should not judge modern zoos based on previous wrongs. Instead, in examining the history of bad zoo practice, we can extract guidance on what makes for a good zoo. Our reference to modern zoos is in part an intention to separate them from the negative associations of earlier practice, while still keeping in mind the lessons of the past.

The first significant shift away from zoos as institutions predominantly for recreation came in the second half of the 20th century. Following the destruction of many European zoos during the Second World War, reconstruction was accompanied by reflections on their ongoing aims. This led to major changes in both their outlook and approach, adding a variety of further goals beyond recreation.[8] Zoos now widely recognize three roles beyond recreation: research, education and conservation, which were added to the goals of zoos in roughly this order. George Rabb – zoologist and director of Chicago's Brookfield Zoo from 1976 to 2003 – represented this evolution from menagerie to zoological park to conservation centre.[9] We argue that now, beyond the conservation centre, zoos should also be aiming to be centres of animal flourishing and throughout this book we will look at what this means in practice.

These aims – recreation, research, conservation and education – are often referred to as the 'four pillars' of modern zoos. Recreation is the entertainment role aimed at providing visitors with a fun and engaging day out, often now associated with deeper connection with zoo animals. Research can refer to any form of knowledge production, whether this involves studies of zoo animals or visitors, and aims to use the unique environment of zoos to promote knowledge. Conservation involves any activities aimed at preserving biodiversity and the natural world, including captive breeding and protection efforts in the wild. Finally, education refers to the goal of teaching zoo visitors about the natural world, species biology and about their own activities as an institution. While we will explore each of these aims in separate chapters, they should be seen as closely intertwined, with the activities and successes in one area potentially feeding into others.

Nevertheless, the goals of zoos can also sometimes come into conflict, raising the question of which goals zoos should prioritize. In this book we will argue that zoos should put the needs of their animals first. Indeed, one of the goals we have for this book is to solidify a growing movement to include animal welfare as a fifth mission or 'pillar' for zoos.[10] It is crucial not to overlook the costs to the animals that may come from meeting those other goals and to continually ensure that zoo animals have high welfare, so that zoos are not only for us but also primarily for other animals. We hope that this book will help to cement the importance of animal welfare as not just one of, but the *central* of the five key goals of zoos.

In this book, we will be discussing and critically evaluating the key roles of zoos, through the 'four pillars' we have already mentioned, to show why and how zoos are for animals. We will begin in Chapter 2 by looking at the aim most closely tied to human interests: that of recreation, and of the importance of facilitating human connection to animals. Chapter 3 turns to the goal of research, its limitations in the zoo setting, and the potential benefits both to animals within the collection and in the wild. Chapter 4 examines the aim of conservation for zoos and shows how zoo conservation encompasses a range of activities beyond just breeding programmes. Linked to this, in Chapter 5 we will discuss the educational role of zoos, and how zoos aim to motivate pro-environmental behaviours, critically analysing to what degree this is successful. Finally, in Chapter 6 the focus is on animal welfare, arguing that it should become the fifth and most important pillar for zoos to ensure that zoos are centrally for animals and not only for us. Chapter 7 will then summarize the argument of this book and outline a positive vision for the future of zoos, including the changes required to realize the vision of zoos that are primarily operating for the good of animals. This will enable us to answer the question of what zoos are for, both in the present and the future.

2
RECREATION: WE'RE GOING TO THE ZOO

The first of the four pillars we will discuss is recreation – the provision of fun or entertainment for the human visitors to the zoo. As mentioned in the Introduction, recreation is the primary reason most people visit zoos. It is also the role that zoo critics have the most problem with, typically viewing zoos as a form of cruel imprisonment for human entertainment. Here, we hope to show that recreation doesn't have to be as problematic as is often assumed. In this chapter and the ones that follow, we will examine the history of the role and how it is currently realized, moving on to examine the potential harms and benefits and finishing with a discussion of whether it can serve to justify the existence of zoos.

History of the recreational role of zoos

Historically, zoos were first developed as menageries: collections of the weird, wonderful and exotic, for the viewing pleasure of those who owned them (typically royal and aristocratic families) and their guests. They were symbols of power and control, where the possession of a range of exotic animals could be seen as a demonstration of one's reach and influence. For instance, for several centuries the Tower of London Menagerie housed an impressive collection of exotic animals that had been gifted to the royal family from their allies and colonies across the world. While there is no strict agreed-upon line dividing menageries and zoos, menageries are often seen as a kind of proto-zoo. Nevertheless, in their status as proto-zoos, these institutions aimed primarily at collecting and displaying as many different species as possible, prizing novelty and rarity. There was little focus given to research and education – not to mention conservation or animal welfare.[1] With almost no knowledge about the needs of the animals they housed, such as their nutritional requirements or preferred environments, most were kept in the same bare cages and fed unnatural foods, such as an elephant belonging to James I who was given a daily drink of wine.

Since early zoos also focused almost exclusively on recreation, it is unsurprising that some have argued that 'zoological gardens are simply sophisticated menageries'.[2] The evolution from early menageries to modern zoos, with their aims of research, conservation and education, was gradual – not a sudden jump as the different terms may suggest. Furthermore, this journey was not merely a matter of adding goals. As well, the aim of recreation itself has changed significantly over the last hundred years.

Today, this recreational role is still going strong. The main reason people visit zoos is still to view animals and have a nice day out with friends or family. Research on zoo visitors has repeatedly shown that visitors are there to have a good time, and that the other aims of a zoo (for example, learning something or helping conservation efforts) are only secondary.[3]

Nevertheless, this recreational role is also the main reason people dislike zoos. As noted in Chapter 1, there is a common perception among zoo abolitionists that zoo animals have been robbed of their freedom and exploited for monetary gain and entertainment. There is an accompanying distaste for the idea of visitors coming in solely to gawk at the animals on display. This visitor–animal interaction is often characterized negatively as people revelling in their sense of superiority over the animals they see: laughing at the 'silly' monkeys or feeling smugly safe at the caging of a previously threatening predator. There is a general concern that the imperialist history of zoos has irrevocably shaped their current form. Beginning as institutions that stood as representations of the wide-reaching global influence and control of those in power over those who served them, could zoos become something other than a place of domination?

Certainly early zoos fed into this image – animals were typically housed in barren exhibits, behind cage bars or often even in pits where people could physically look down upon them, without escape from the gaze of visitors (Figure 2.1). These allowed the animals to be easily seen and have been read as a symbol of human dominion over nature, where visitors were permitted or even encouraged to throw food or other objects at the animals. Similarly, animals were often used for controversial performances such as chimpanzee tea parties (Box 2.1) or elephant rides for the entertainment of visitors – practices that are now only found in non-accredited zoos.

Figure 2.1: A 'bear pit' at the Jardin des Plantes, Paris (1906)

Box 2.1: Janie the tea party chimp

Janie was a chimpanzee who lived at Auckland Zoo from 1956 until her death in 2013, and one who Heather had the privilege of spending time with (Figures 2.2 and 2.3). She was captured from Sierra Leone as an infant and taken to New Zealand, where she lived with three other chimps who were collectively known as the 'tea party chimps'. They would take part in shows where they were dressed up in human clothes and sat at little tables to have 'tea parties' for the entertainment of visitors. These shows stopped in 1964 in response to changing attitudes, but the chimps continued to live at the zoo. Janie was the last survivor and Heather met her in 2005, around a year after the death of her last companion, Bobbie. Because of Janie's unusual early upbringing and lack of proper chimpanzee socialization, she wasn't able to live with other chimps, and so her keepers became her primary companions. Working with Janie meant spending a lot of dedicated time with her, and providing a variety of activities – such as painting or puzzle feeders – to keep her occupied. She had a small TV set and loved watching videos of other animals at the zoo, getting especially excited when she saw her favourite keepers on screen. She was beloved by all her keepers, but the challenges of her care illustrate the lasting harm arising from hand-raising animals for such performances.

Figure 2.2: Janie with her fellow 'tea party' chimpanzees

Figure 2.3: Janie in 2005

While these sorts of practices have created many of the calls for abolition of zoos, modern zoos have moved far from this model and work hard to present animals in a more respectful, natural setting. As early as the late 19th century, Carl Hagenbeck pioneered naturalistic 'cageless' enclosures using moats as barriers, displaying animals in a panoramic fashion as they may be seen in the wild (Figure 2.4).[4] Here animals could be seen without bars, on the same eye level as visitors, and ideally with places to hide.

Figure 2.4: Exhibit at the Tierpark Hagenbeck

Carl Hagenbeck opened the Tierpark Hagenbeck in Hamburg in 1907, famous for open-plan multi-species vistas such as this one

However, one cannot deny the darker history of zoos. One of the most disturbing practices in zoo history was the inclusion of humans in so-called 'human zoos' where 'primitive' people were held captive and publicly displayed to feed the curiosity and feelings of superiority of White Europeans. While this practice is now universally condemned, it raises the important question of whether there is a relevant parallel with our treatment of animals today. Is their display similarly unacceptable? Will we morally condemn animal zoos in the future just as we do human zoos today? Are modern zoos used to show our superiority over other animals and encourage a kind of human exceptionalism in just the same way that human zoos promoted racist attitudes and behaviour? The recreational role of zoos is thus the most potentially problematic and one that deserves scrutiny. What are some of the potential harms to animals that arise from this role and how might modern zoos minimize or prevent them?

Potential harms from recreation

The main criticism of the recreational role of zoos is the potential harms caused to animals. We see two ways in which zoo animals could be harmed by being on display to visitors. The first is through the nature of the relationship that zoos may promote between humans and animals: one of domination and human superiority. The second is through the more direct welfare harms animals may experience from being subject to constant human gaze. The more fundamental challenge – that animals are intrinsically harmed simply by being held in captivity, regardless of display – we will return to in Chapter 6.

Whether or not zoos promote a relationship of domination and attitudes of human superiority is a difficult question to answer. Animals are certainly being held captive, under human control. There is an obvious asymmetry of power between zoo animals and the human staff and visitors. Having large groups of people watching the animals, particularly if they are standing over them, could subconsciously reinforce messages of dominance. In the most extreme form of this argument, ethicist Ralph Acampora has compared zoos with pornography, in the way that this kind of viewing can imply 'mastery and control'.[5] He believes the zoo experience to impart the message that animals exist for mere human entertainment.

Zoo visitors who see the purpose of the zoo solely as entertainment do appear to have less empathy for the animals and are potentially more likely to engage in negative behaviours towards the animals they see.[6] For instance, sometimes visitors can become frustrated when they are not able to easily view the animals they have come to see. This can lead to visitors shouting at animals, banging on windows, crossing barriers and throwing objects at animals, which is surprisingly common among both children and adults[7] and could be seen as reflecting attitudes of domination. It is thus unsurprising that there is a lot of literature on zoos as centres of domination at which humans experience and exhibit their power over animals, or even nature itself.[8]

However, many of these behaviours may actually reflect a desire to make a connection with animals through provoking a response that requires the animal to acknowledge the visitor's presence, rather than simply a disregard for their interests. If zoos can educate their visitors about the animals, presenting them as agents with their own interests – that may not include being active or performing for viewers – this could help reduce negative visitor behaviours and improve animal welfare. It's likely that attitudes of human superiority are built outside of the zoo and brought in by visitors, rather than created there. Here zoos could have an important role in shifting the public perception of animals as creatures that matter for their own sake and that people should feel privileged to see. In the words of a zoo educator: 'We are in the animal's home, and not the other way around.'[9] When visitors come with this mindset, they will be much less likely to engage in these bad behaviours.

Furthermore, modern zoos work hard to create in visitors a feeling of awe at seeing the animals, not one of power or dominion. Research into the effects of exhibit design on visitor perceptions suggests that immersive and naturalistic exhibits elicit more respect and appreciation for zoo animals.[10] So while bad zoos may contribute to attitudes of human superiority and domination, this does not suggest that the same would be true for good zoos, which aim instead at influencing people to care about animals (both in the zoo and in the wild).

Another potential source of harm comes from being on display. This could be instrumentally bad (reducing animal welfare by, for example, negative feelings coming from being unable to hide) or intrinsically bad through undermining their dignity, regardless of whether or not this impacts their welfare. The philosopher Simon Coghlan, for instance, argues that violations of animal dignity are intrinsic harms, irreducible to their instrumental effects.[11] Dignity is tied to recognition of the intrinsic worth of another being and their right as an autonomous agent to not be treated as a mere means. While there might be some intuitive appeal to this idea, we are quite sceptical of the intrinsic version of this argument for several reasons.

Notably, the concept of dignity was originally used in an anthropocentric way to assign humans unique moral worth (whether coming from our higher rational or cognitive faculties, or other features) that animals lack. Philosophers such as Peter Singer have therefore criticized the notion of dignity as speciesist, representing a form of prejudice against species other than our own.[12] Others are sceptical whether the concept of dignity makes sense at all, or is useful to adopt even in the human case.[13] The case for valuing dignity in animals is even more difficult to make, as most nonhuman animals will not have the capacity to conceptualize or value their own dignity, lacking any desire for respectful treatment over and above its impacts on their own welfare. Many thus dismiss animal dignity as an incoherent concept and instead take the value of dignity to reduce to other properties, such as natural flourishing or wellbeing.[14] The concern is that views advocating for the intrinsic value of dignity are merely projections of human attitudes and preferences about our own treatment onto other species who have no such concern.

Nevertheless, we can still grant that animals can be harmed by the ways they are presented and viewed. It is just that these harms are instrumental welfare harms, rather than intrinsic. Similar to most humans, many animals may dislike being constantly watched, being too close to others or exposed to constant noise, without any places to retreat to.

While life in a zoo can expose animals to these experiences, it doesn't have to. Zoos are taking very seriously the question of whether animals suffer direct welfare harms from being on public display. There is now a wide range of studies examining the 'visitor effects' on different species.[15] The lockdowns that occurred as a result of the COVID-19 pandemic also provided an ideal opportunity for zoos to study the change in the behaviour of their animals when visitors were suddenly absent.[16] Perhaps unsurprisingly, the results have been mixed. Some species, such as elephants and kangaroos, seemed more relaxed with visitors absent, some, like meerkats and capuchins, became bored and required additional enrichment and interactions of other kinds and some, such as bears, appeared indifferent. There is thus no clear-cut characterization of the effect of zoo visitors on animals, with many different environmental and animal-based variables influencing the effect.[17] We cannot say that being on display is simply a good or a bad thing for animals, but rather that it depends on specific features of the situation.

It's important that zoos pay attention to the results of studies like these and use them to guide choices about which species to keep and how to house them. Some species that strongly dislike visitor presence should perhaps not be included in zoo collections at all. Others could be housed in ways that minimize this impact, such as having more areas to retreat to, or viewing only through smaller 'peepholes' rather than along large stretches of their habitat. Zoos can build complex enclosures with shelters to offer animals opportunities to escape from the human gaze, giving them sufficient space and the choice of privacy when they want it. For animals who are more attuned to the sounds and scents in their environment than the visual, more creative design ideas may be needed to help them retreat from the additional sensory burden visitors create. This can help provide them with agency to protect their own interests, as we would often associate with respect for dignity in humans. So long as animal welfare and interests are prioritized, we can resist the common complaint that zoo animals are treated as a mere means rather than ends in themselves.

For those who remain committed to the intrinsic value of animal dignity, it still seems entirely possible for zoo animals to be respected as subjects, with their needs and agency valued, and for this to be made apparent to the visiting public. Zoos should take this seriously by considering how they present their animals and how this may influence public attitudes as well as the potential dignity of the animals. To do so is important whether one takes the harms of disrespect to be intrinsic, or merely instrumental, as we do. Some zoos even explicitly recognize the importance of animal dignity, such as the Taronga Conservation Society Australia, which specifically describes in their animal welfare charter a commitment 'to provide dignity, respect and the best care for our animals'.[18] This includes an intention to maintain dignity in the way animals are presented and how they interact with visitors during encounters and keeper presentations. Indeed, zoos probably do better in this respect than do many other human interactions with animals. If we compare the care and housing of zoo animals to other forms of animal captivity, zoos recognize the individuality of the animal in a way that is missing in most other contexts.

While there are potential harms arising from the exhibition of zoo animals, a carefully designed and well-run zoo should be able to offset or prevent these harms. Shifting from the question of whether this is harmful to animals, we can now investigate what recreational benefits zoos can provide.

Recreational benefits

Few will deny that zoos are fun to visit. There are many sources of joy that they can provide, from watching a favourite animal, to discovering new species, to being surprised at the animals' behaviour, to interacting more closely with them. But what makes them uniquely entertaining over other ways of spending free time?

In particular, if we are asking whether zoos can be justified, we have to consider what they can provide over and above experiences such as watching wildlife documentaries. We see the critical difference in the role of facilitating a connection with the animals visitors encounter. In reading zoos as a place where people come to connect with animals, rather than passively view them, we can move from interpreting zoos as a demonstration of human dominion over animals to an expression of respect for and empathy with them.

So far we have presented the interactions between animals and visitors as one of mere viewing. Indeed, critical discussion of zoos often focuses on the role of vision and the ways that animals are visually presented.[19] However, this fails to completely capture the zoo experience. Instead of going to zoos to just *view* animals, there is a sense in which visitors want to *experience* and *connect* with animals. This experience works through senses other than just vision. There is something important that arises from being there in person – from sharing their space, and experiencing their presence and actions through all of our senses. From Heather's zookeeping experience, it is apparent that visitors want more out of their visits than just to look at the animals. They appear to seek out special connections and interactions with animals that make visiting the zoo worthwhile.

It seems undeniable that humans have an innate love of and desire for connection with the natural world. Biologist E.O. Wilson popularized the term 'biophilia' to describe this phenomenon, arguing that humans have a deeply rooted love or affinity for the biological world.[20] This creates an urge to seek connections with members of other species, which can explain the popularity of zoos as one of the few places such connections can be found.

Novelist and critic John Berger, in his essay 'Why Look at Animals?', describes the connection visitors seek from zoos: to meet the gaze of a member of another species and feel that one is simultaneously observing and observed, to recapture a type of encounter that has been lost as animals disappeared from our daily lives.[21] It is these unique recreational benefits we need to look at in order to assess whether zoos are justified, because the connection that arises from meeting an animal there may have elements that aren't possible to capture in alternative modes of experiencing animals, such as watching videos.

It is notable that the advent of wildlife documentaries, while allowing people to see wild animals in a more authentic way, has not decreased the popularity of zoos – in fact it has, if anything, increased it. This suggests that there is something that people are getting from a zoo experience that they can't get from watching a documentary; something beyond merely seeing the animal in a video – the experience of meeting it (Box 2.2). Visitors themselves report that their primary motive in visiting zoos is to *be with* animals.[22]

Zoo visitors viewing and interacting with animals can have positive feelings, such as connection, awe and respect. They will have a more positive reaction to the animals they see when they are able to see the animals

Box 2.2: Connecting with a seal

We recently visited the Melbourne Zoo in Australia and while we were there, we were struck by the goings-on at the fur seal exhibit. This exhibit has a large underwater viewing window, that had drawn a large crowd. When we got closer, we could see that one of the seals was down in the water, on the other side of the window, playing with the visitors. The seal would hover in the water, eye to eye with a visitor (usually a child) and as the child would wave a bag or a jacket around in the air, the seal would follow it in loops and somersaults, before returning to wait for the next round. Occasionally surfacing for quick breaths, the seal chose to spend the rest of her time down with the people. It was obvious how enthralled everyone was by this – us included. The room was quiet and people were pressed as close as they could to the window, wanting the opportunity to connect. Although most exhibits hold visitor attention for a few minutes at most, many of these people remained for at least the 30 minutes we were down there. To us this was a strong testament to just how powerful the connections people make with zoo animals can be. We have no doubt that this is a memory all of them will carry with them for the rest of their lives.

up close, witness some of their behaviours, or observe husbandry procedures such as feeding or training sessions where the animals are trained to perform behaviours that can assist their husbandry and medical care.[23] The popularity of 'behind the scenes' and similar experiences where visitors can, for instance, feed the animals speak to this desire, and these experiences are becoming increasingly common offerings from zoos.

In line with this, many zoos are now trying to broaden their recreational role to a focus on 'connection' or 'engagement'. The aim is to encourage people not to see a visit to the zoo as merely a fun day out to look at animals, in the same way one might go to see a movie. Instead, the desire is to encourage people to really connect with the animals they see, as individual subjects. For instance, some zoos place signs that name the animals in the exhibit, or describe their personalities. We recently visited the Oceanarium at Bournemouth, which described each of their penguins on signs around the exhibit – both their looks and personalities – and it encouraged us to spend time trying to identify each of them. This provides visitors with a sense of 'knowing' the animals that you wouldn't necessarily have from simply viewing them at a single moment in time.

Regular visitors often get to know animals by name and their specific habits, such as a couple frequently observed by Heather when she worked at the Taronga Western Plains Zoo. They would visit the Siamang Island on a weekly basis, to have lunch with the family of siamangs (a type of gibbon). They knew all the animals by name, as well as their birthdays, and could interpret much of the animals' communicative behaviour. This certainly indicates a desire for individual connection and this sense of connection may be one of the strongest benefits zoos provide – both for humans and for other animals.

Anthropologist Juno Salazar Parreñas describes the importance of 'co-presence', 'to feel that they are part of something, [visitors] have to be there in the flesh, to feel things on the surface of their skin and on a specific surface of the earth'.[24] Zoos allow a co-presence that can connect people to animals in a unique way. The importance of in-person presence has been made especially salient in recent years, with most people finding that online video calls are no replacement for meeting family, friends or coworkers in person. Viewing animals in the wild is not financially viable for most, and if pursued to excess can lead to ecosystem damage and negative impacts on the animals. For most zoo visitors, zoos provide the best opportunity to experience the presence of animals they would otherwise never encounter.

People who participate in up-close interactions, such as swimming with dolphins, report a sense of attachment to the animals they meet.[25] Up-close animal encounters are often seen as a special occasion, frequently used as a birthday or anniversary present, for example. Some encounters allow humans to touch the animals, utilizing the social aspect of the tactile sense. Touching requires two participants, as opposed to, say, smelling or seeing, which can be done in isolation. It is an intimate form of contact, requiring close proximity, and implies acceptance and even affection. As opposed to the subject–object division that is created with vision, if people desire to meet animals, it is a subject–subject connection they seek. The presence of a second subject is what differentiates the experience from, for example, that of a museum or documentary. This subject has the power to continue the interaction or to end it.

It is also worth noting that the benefits of connection to animals aren't just for the visitors – zookeepers also often form close and valuable bonds with the animals in their care. Research has found that this can serve as a positive source of joy, comfort and wellbeing, and forms a large part of their job satisfaction,[26] compensating for less desirable aspects of the job such as low pay and tough, often dirty, physical work. Different zoo cultures will encourage or discourage such relationships to varying degrees, but the animals themselves can also benefit from these bonds (see Chapter 6).

Zoos undoubtedly provide benefits to humans who view and experience the animals, benefits that go beyond mere recreation. These connections may also increase the benefits associated with other zoo goals, such as education and conservation, as we will discuss in later chapters. But is this enough?

Does recreation justify the existence of zoos?

The biggest question about the recreational role of zoos is whether such benefits to humans are sufficient to justify their existence, and whether these could outweigh potential harms to animals. In our view, the recreational benefits of zoos are not alone sufficiently weighty to justify their existence. While this is a source of human wellbeing, it is not one that is fundamental to living a good life, and it is one that can in principle be replaced by other leisure activities. Even if we take the deeper role of connection we have just discussed, this is still at its core a benefit to human wellbeing.

While connection to members of other species is valuable to many people, it is not sufficient to justify use of animals in cases where those animals might be harmed. Animal collections that only aimed at the entertainment of humans without regard for animal welfare are certainly not justified. However, recreation does not necessarily come at a cost of harm to animals. Where this is true and animals are kept well, zoos may hold a mild justification for their existence in the connection of humans to animals, as they are one of the few places that can facilitate such connections. However, we see the main benefits of this role in the strong instrumental value.

The recreational role is deeply tied to the economics of zoos – running a zoo is an expensive exercise in terms of staffing and animal care. A worry from zoo critics is that these concerns will drive the business model of zoos, to the exclusion of the other goals they may claim to pursue. In this view, zoos will focus on providing an entertaining spectacle that visitors will keep paying to come and see, regardless of the costs to the animals. However, this view seems too pessimistic – both about the motivations of zoos (many of which are partially government-funded or non-profit organizations) and of zoo visitors. There is growing evidence that public sentiment is in support of animal welfare and conservation aims (even more so among those who typically visit zoos)[27] and institutions that do not do well in these regards are unlikely to attract sufficient visitors to continue operations in the long term. Here, then, there will be at least partial alignment between the economic and other goals of zoos.

For most zoos (especially those without council or government funding), admission fees cover the largest part of their operating budgets, relying on the recreational role – and particularly that of connection – to bring in visitors. Zoos depend on visitors to continue running and to carry out the other operations we will look at throughout the book. The financial difficulties faced by many institutions during the COVID-19 pandemic shutdowns illustrate just how important visitor revenue is to continuing operations, including the provision of high welfare conditions for the animals. It also brings in visitors, whose attention can be directed to some of the education and conservation aims. This provides additional justification for a focus on recreation in zoos.

Conclusion

Zoos are most popular for their role as sites of recreation, particularly in facilitating meaningful connections between human visitors and the animals they encounter. These are benefits to humans, and thus don't contribute to our claim that zoos are primarily for animals. However, they have flow-on effects that benefit animals, such as through raising funds to support animal care and other zoo activities, and when the connection felt by visitors inspires conservation action. Zoo visits may also help promote a more positive attitude towards animals, so long as the animals are presented carefully and respectfully. However, zoos need to work to prevent or minimize any harms caused to animals from viewing by or interaction with visitors.

While the recreational role of zoos is not for the animals in a direct sense, it can be managed to ensure it is not causing harm to animals, and that it can provide indirect benefits to the animals – both those in the zoo and those in the wild. The recreational role of zoos is not alone sufficient to justify their existence, but may serve as some smaller source of value alongside the other roles we will go on to discuss – research, education, conservation and animal welfare.

3
RESEARCH:
LEARNING FROM
THE ANIMALS

oving beyond recreation, the next rationale often presented for the existence of zoos is research. This is the second-oldest aim for zoos, with some of the earliest parks serving as research institutions that helped to advance scientific progress. Since then, zoo research has only continued to expand, such as can be seen through the work of the late well-known primatologist and ethologist Frans de Waal, who wrote several popular books on his experiences and work with chimpanzees at Burgers' Zoo in Arnhem, Netherlands and the Yerkes National Primate Research Center. But what are the different types of research that are conducted in zoos, and can these serve to justify their existence?

History of zoo research

The first formal appearance of a scientific zoo dates back to the establishment of the Zoological Society of London in 1826, which opened its gates to fellows of the Zoological Society in 1828 with the explicit goal of advancing the study of zoology. What is now known as London Zoo only opened to the public in 1847, demonstrating that the recreation aim has not always come first. When we lived in London, we were frequent visitors to the London Zoo, and were surprised to learn through its displays how integral research was to its mission and what a big role it played in its history. For instance, Charles Darwin, who developed and championed the theory of evolution by natural selection, was himself a fellow of the society. His time spent observing the behaviour of animals in their zoo strongly influenced his theorizing (Figure 3.1).

Figure 3.1: Jenny the orangutan at London Zoo

Jenny was the first orangutan housed in London Zoo. In 1838 Charles Darwin visited her, the first time he'd seen a great ape in person. His reflections on her similarities to human children shaped his views on the continuity between humans and other animals.

The learned society dedicated to zoology allowed scientists to conduct observations of animals that otherwise would have required long and difficult journeys to exotic places, as well as bringing them into contact with a larger number of different species. While it is now recognized that animals in captivity often behave differently from those in the wild, meaning this cannot serve to replace field observations, zoos continue to play an important role as centres of animal research.

The field of zoo biology was formally defined in the 1960s by the biologist Heini Hediger[1] and in recent decades has progressed rapidly. Some large zoos have their own research centres, publishing numerous scientific publications per year, such as the Smithsonian's National Zoo and Conservation Biology Institute, the Taronga Institute for Science and Learning in Sydney, Australia, and the Institute of Zoology at the Zoological Society of London. Unfortunately, this is the exception rather than the rule, especially across the larger number of smaller institutions.

A major obstacle to animal research in zoos since their beginnings has been the lack of zoo scientists. Compared to universities, many zoos are also chronically underfunded, making investments into research typically sparse. Many zoos have dealt with this problem by developing close collaborations with universities or university researchers. For instance, the German Max Planck Institute for Evolutionary Anthropology has cooperated with Leipzig Zoo to create the Wolfgang Köhler Primate Research Center.

Similarly, the University of Sydney has teamed up with the Taronga Conservation Society Australia (which runs both the Taronga Zoo in Sydney and Taronga Western Plains Zoo in central New South Wales) to offer a joint degree focusing on conservation. Such collaborations and partnerships allow university staff and students access to animals and enclosures, or records and samples. This provides mutual benefit, with university researchers gaining access to animals they would not otherwise be able to study, and zoos getting the benefits of research expertise and access to technology to answer questions they are interested in for their collections.

Of course, these collaborations also create their own challenges. Research has shown that it can be hard to align the differences in goals and institutional culture between the different types of institutions.[2] For instance, researchers may have difficulties understanding that zoo operations may limit the types of changes they can make for experimental purposes. Here it is important to make room for ongoing communication to ensure productive and long-lasting research cooperations.

Moving beyond in-house research, zoos also have the opportunity to contribute to larger research projects involving zoos worldwide. This can include donating samples to biobanks to make them available to researchers for a range of comparative projects, as well as entering animal and husbandry data on the worldwide record-keeping tool ZIMS (Zoological Information Management Software) to create an enormous database that – while primarily used for knowledge exchange between zoos – can also be applied to research. Initiatives such as the ManyZoos project allow zoos to connect their research efforts and increase the impact of research from individual zoos that on their own would have insufficiently large sample sizes.[3]

Today, research has become one of the core goals of many zoos across the world. The European Association of Zoos and Aquaria (EAZA) requires all accredited member zoos to participate in research activities, with a set of standards in place to guide their research.[4] EAZA has even developed its own open access journal (the *Journal of Zoo and Aquarium Research*) for easier publication and widespread dissemination of research results. Together with the German Association of Zoological Gardens, EAZA also launched the Zoo Science Library as a digital collection of zoo research across the world.[5] The database is accessible to all members, which as well as allowing zoos to benefit from the research of others, also serves to quantify and characterize the existing and ongoing zoo research.

Types of zoo research

There are three primary types of research undertaken in zoos. The first is research aimed at the operations of zoos: largely research into the biology and husbandry of zoo animals. The second type is more fundamental investigations into animal behaviour, biology, physiology and ecology for better understanding of the species and in some cases for conservation purposes. While research in the first and second categories can overlap, they are differentiated by their goals. Finally, there is research into animal cognition. We will briefly introduce all three types here before we move on to the question of whether any of them could serve to justify zoos.

The first category – research into zoo animal husbandry – is the most common type of zoo research.[6] This research includes their environmental needs, nutrition, behaviour, reproduction, health care and welfare, which then guide evidence-based best practice animal care. There are dedicated journals for this type of research, such as *Zoo Biology* (founded in 1982) and the *Journal of Zoo and Aquarium Research* (since 2013). Other research can positively influence welfare through looking at how animals use their enclosures, where they spend their time, finding out which food types or other resources they prefer, determining how to successfully integrate new or unusual social groupings, or evaluating the success of enrichment activities. Collection of demographic, genetic and reproductive data for zoo 'studbooks' that guide population management can also be usefully applied to research questions. This sort of research can help challenge established wisdom in animal husbandry, such as showing that animals like tigers that were believed to be solitary can do well when housed in small social groups.[7] While there are still many understudied species[8] and a strong mammal-centric bias, zoo researchers are now working to fill evidence gaps, focusing on unexplored and less charismatic species such as cockroaches.[9]

In addition to animal research, the category of zoo operational research also features human research using the social sciences. This can examine questions such as the success of education and conservation initiatives and attitudes of zoo visitors. Understanding the motivations of zoo visitors is crucial for determining how to positively influence them and how to improve zoos to better meet their goals of entertaining and educating visitors.

The next most common type of research in zoos aims at developing general foundational knowledge of species, in particular their behaviour, biology, physiology and ecology. There is some natural overlap with the research described earlier. Learning about zoo animals and identifying their needs requires learning about the species more generally. However, this research can be done without any specific husbandry aim in mind. For animals that are difficult to observe in the wild – particularly rare or cryptic species – captive specimens can be studied to learn about their behaviour and life history (for example, growth rate, gestation duration, litter size). Some of this research is also valuable for conservation purposes – in learning about the genetics or reproduction of endangered species that are being bred in captivity, for example, or in developing or testing techniques for monitoring wild animals.

Finally, we have animal cognition research. This is used both to better understand the cognitive abilities of different animals (that can then sometimes have applications in welfare or conservation) and to make inferences about the evolution of cognitive processes. Cognitive research looks at abilities such as learning, tool-making, cooperation, memory, numerical abilities and problem-solving. Though animal cognition studies have typically taken place in laboratory settings, we argue that animals in zoos provide a useful (and currently underutilized) resource for this research. The purchase and maintenance of laboratory animals is expensive, which has typically led to a narrow focus on a small number of species such as corvids and primates. Zoos, however, hold a wide range of species and the animals are easy to access, habituated to human presence, and researchers are able to control their environment to some degree, allowing them to conduct experimental studies. A 2021 review found that almost 25 per cent of primate cognition research has taken place in zoos, with a greater range of species diversity than laboratory research.[10] Cognition research in zoos has allowed work on species that are unlikely to be studied in any other context (see Box 3.1 for an example). Because such research can help us to understand the nature of cognitive and mental faculties beyond just the species under investigation, and especially the human mind, it holds a lot of value and is potentially one of the best ways zoos could use their collections to contribute to research outcomes.

Box 3.1: Cooperating porcupines

African crested porcupines are cooperative breeders that form lifelong pairs, such as the pair housed at the Creature Conservancy in Michigan, USA (Figure 3.2). This pair – named Bedhead and Lady Gaga – was recruited for a study looking at cooperative behaviour in the species. This was tested using a string-pulling task requiring both porcupines to work together to obtain a food reward. The testing showed that though both animals quickly learned how to perform the task, they didn't show any special responsiveness to the actions of their partner that would suggest deliberate cooperation.[11] Their usually shy nature and complex housing requirements mean they would be difficult to study in the wild or a laboratory and so the captive pair provided a perfect opportunity to learn more about social cognition in these unusual creatures.

Overall, zoos have the potential to support a wide range of research activities with a unique set of benefits and drawbacks and can serve as a useful complement to other types of research, such as laboratory experiments and field observations. Zoos allow for more control over conditions than field work, though with a narrower scope. They also have a more diverse range of species and greater ecological validity than laboratory research, but with more potential confounds (additional variables that can influence the results of a study). Comparisons between captive and

Figure 3.2: African crested porcupines Bedhead and Lady Gaga cooperating on a string-pulling task to access food

wild animals can demonstrate types of behavioural flexibility and population variation. Observations from captive animals may also identify previously unknown phenomena of interest to go out and study in the wild. Zoo research is thus best seen as a contributing piece within a larger research agenda. However, the question still remains whether research outputs can justify the existence of zoos – is this a significant part of what zoos are for?

Does research justify zoos?

To consider whether the research undertaken in zoos is valuable enough to justify their existence, we will examine each of the types in turn. Beginning with zoo-facing research, this plainly cannot justify zoos. After all, it is beneficial only given the existence of zoos; it is not an independent benefit provided by them. While it is undoubtedly important to have research into the best ways to house and care for zoo animals and to ensure their welfare, it is not of independent value. An important exception to this is when the husbandry information can be used to conduct successful breeding and release programmes for endangered species where captive breeding programmes are their best option for continued survival, or to improve housing and husbandry of rescued animals undergoing rehabilitation for re-release.

Moving to the second category of more foundational biological research, a much stronger case for zoos can be made. Field research is difficult to conduct and potentially stressful for wild animals unfamiliar with humans. However, there are also important limitations to zoo research. In particular, the unusual rearing and living conditions (when compared to their wild counterparts) can reduce the external validity of zoo research (that is, how much it tells us about the species in general, rather than merely the members living in captivity). The small number of animals of any given species living in a zoo also reduces the statistical power of any studies undertaken. Multi-institution studies that take a larger number of animals across a wide range of living conditions may fare better, but all the animals are still going to differ to some extent from their wild counterparts.

There is a trade-off here between ease of access and quality of results and zoo research could never replace the study of animals in the wild. However, we still see a role for the semi-natural conditions of zoos to serve as a complement to and bridge between laboratory and field research. This can then offer a partial justification for the existence of zoos, both for human reasons, where one values the gain in such knowledge, and benefits to animals arising from the potential applications in conservation and animal welfare. The caveat here is that this is still not a widespread form of research in zoos and to properly serve as justification for them, there would need to be a bigger shift in (or expansion of) zoo research from pure husbandry-based studies to this more foundational biological exploration.

Turning lastly to animal cognition research, it is here that zoos have the potential for a strong and unique contribution. They can provide access to a vast range of animals under conditions suited for research aimed at progressing our understanding of the mind. As most of this research is currently performed in laboratories, zoos could serve as a more naturalistic and ecologically valid location for cognition research, without the difficulties associated with trying to study cognitive abilities in wild populations – especially in allowing for long-term studies of individuals or groups that would be difficult to achieve in the wild.

Nevertheless, the same caution mentioned earlier also needs to apply here. While the abilities demonstrated by an animal in a zoo certainly represent what a member of their species is capable of, it may not represent the normal abilities shown by a wild member of the species. Particularly for great apes, enculturation to humans during their rearing may alter their brains, behaviour and abilities in ways that limit the informativeness about 'normal' wild individuals. There are also concerns about small sample sizes (which can be partially offset by multi-institutional studies, though differences between sites need to be taken into account) and lack of full control over environmental variables, where husbandry and welfare priorities can override research concerns.

As compared to research subjects housed in laboratory conditions, though, we want to emphasize again that zoos potentially provide a higher-welfare (and more ecologically valid) alternative for cognition research. Participation in research could even itself be enriching for the animal, as demonstrated in research on dolphins showing they engaged in more playful and social behaviours on days they were tested.[12] Research could also provide insights into suitable cognitive enrichment for zoo-housed species, such as puzzle feeders and other intellectually challenging tasks.[13] This research therefore has potential value both for humans, allowing us to better understand the minds of ourselves and others, and for animals, who can benefit from this understanding. For this reason, cognition seems like the sort of research that can best justify zoos; though again this requires a greater dedication of attention and resources to this goal.

Conclusion

Zoos can support a range of unique research activities that provide at least a partial justification for their existence and, importantly, benefits that are largely for the animals. While animal research is often viewed critically, most zoo research is aimed at the animals themselves. Animal husbandry research directly benefits the animals housed, as it can lead to ongoing improvements in their care. Learning about animal behaviour and ecology can be useful for implementing conservation programmes that help wild species. And animal cognition research may help both humans and animals. As humans, we often use data on animal cognition to help better understand our own minds. However, knowing more about the mental abilities of animals can also help encourage respect for them. People's empathy for animals is related to their perception of the intelligence and sentience of the animals, and so the more we know about what they are capable of, the more we can appeal to the sentiments of those who we want to protect them. A deeper knowledge of the minds of other animals can build a greater appreciation of them as individual subjects, leading to increased moral consideration and better treatment. Understanding what their minds are like also helps to understand their interests and provide better lives.

However, to truly realize the vision of the scientific 'empirical zoo',[14] many zoos need to make some improvements or shifts in focus. These include all accredited zoos making an effort to participate in research activities to whatever degree they are able. This could include building collaborations with local universities, participating in multi-zoo research projects or even setting up dedicated on-site research centres. Zoos should focus on those areas they have the capacity to do best in, including husbandry, cognition research and conservation research co-created with in situ conservation partners based on their needs. By doing this, zoos can increase the benefits they provide to both humans and animals.

4
CONSERVATION: BEYOND THE ARK

Perhaps the primary role that modern zoos themselves highlight is conservation. Indeed, the general public perceive conservation as zoos' most important role.[1] This is potentially the strongest justification for zoos, as almost everyone agrees that protecting the natural world is a high priority. However, some zoo critics argue that zoos do poorly in their conservation efforts.[2] How do zoos actually contribute to conservation, and do their conservation activities justify their continuing existence?

History of zoo conservation

When zoos first started focusing on conservation initiatives, the most commonly used metaphor was that of the ark – made explicit in books like *Ethics on the Ark* and *After the Ark?* Zoos were seen as centres of preservation, like a living gene bank where endangered animals could be held while their habitats and wild relatives were disappearing.

Throughout the 1980s and 1990s, discussion of zoo conservation increased and the importance of their educational role was also recognized. Following the 1992 Earth Summit in Rio de Janeiro that gave rise to the Convention of Biodiversity, the World Association of Zoos and Aquariums worked with the International Union for the Conservation of Nature to produce a World Zoo Conservation Strategy, which has since been updated twice.[3] In the 21st century, conservation has become ever more important and many zoos have been renamed and rebranded as 'conservation parks' with the aim of preventing species from going extinct. Jenny Gray, Chief Executive Officer of Zoos Victoria, described zoos' journey from the morally dubious institutions arising during colonial times to the conservation 'heroes' of today as 'a story of redemption'.[4] Now, zoos undertake a broad range of conservation initiatives, understanding the conservation role as helping the natural world in a more general sense, with use of all the resources at their disposal. Some zoos even house their own conservation organizations, such as the Auckland Zoo Conservation Fund and the Ocean Conservation Trust at the National Marine Aquarium in Plymouth, UK.

Conservation has become a global priority. The preservation of the natural world and prevention of environmental degradation impact everyone on the planet, human and nonhuman alike. The

UN Convention on Biological Diversity expresses a commitment to preservation of diversity, and sustainable and equitable use of global resources. In 2022, this included adoption of the Kunming-Montreal Global Biodiversity Framework, which sets a range of biodiversity targets to meet by 2030.[5] Of most relevance to zoos is Target 4, which asks for in situ and ex situ conservation efforts to manage species to reduce extinction risk and conserve species and genetic diversity. In situ refers to on-site conservation projects occurring where species are threatened, while ex situ are off-site projects taking place away from the original habitat. Zoos are also well placed to help meet Target 16, which relates to promoting and facilitating sustainable consumer behaviour, and the enabling conditions relating to raising awareness and appreciation of biodiversity. Here, we will bracket off this education role until the next chapter and first focus on how zoos work with ex situ and in situ conservation.

Ex situ conservation

When people think about zoos' conservation role, they are most likely to have in mind conservation breeding – housing and breeding endangered animals, with the intention of releasing to replenish wild stocks. Zoos themselves perpetuate this image, with large media campaigns surrounding the births of threatened species. Even many zookeepers will describe their primary contributions to conservation through these programmes. However, we take this role to be only a minor part of the value of zoos for conservation.

There have been some notable successes for conservation breeding within zoos: species that were previously endangered or even extinct in the wild have been successfully reintroduced from captive-bred populations. The Przewalski's horse (or takhi), the Australian Corroboree frog, the Arabian oryx, the golden lion tamarin, the California condor, the Bermuda snail and the black-footed ferret are among the most high-profile cases. Particularly for the species classified as 'extinct in the wild' (that is, individuals remaining only in captivity), ex situ conservation will be the only option if they are not to be lost forever. As many as two-thirds of birds and mammals that have been saved from extinction over the past few decades are thought to have been helped by ex situ conservation efforts.[6]

Zoos have the potential to provide a valuable service for the protection of threatened species when their wild populations are at risk, with the resources and expertise to mobilize quickly. Holding 'insurance' populations that can be used in response to natural disasters or similar events can help prevent catastrophic species declines (Box 4.1). This may indeed be the best use of the 'ark' populations zoos hold.

However, despite these successes, most species held in zoos will never be reintroduced into the wild, nor is that the intention. Reintroducing animals is difficult and costly, with a high failure rate.[7] Extensive training and quarantine are needed (to prevent transmission of

Box 4.1: Saving Tasmanian devils

Tasmanian devils are an iconic Australian species, recently threatened by a transmissible cancer called Devil Facial Tumour Disease. This spreads between devils when they gather to feed at carcasses and causes such large growths on the face and mouth that eventually they are no longer able to eat and starve to death (Figure 4.1). The disease caused a rapid decline of the wild population – around an 80 per cent loss over two decades.[8] While research efforts were under way to find treatments or a cure, through a partnership of a local zoo body, non-governmental organization and government department, over one hundred wild Tasmanian devils were taken into captivity to protect them from contracting the disease and create a disease-free insurance population. While some were taken into specially built sanctuaries, many were housed in zoos. With a short lifespan and fast breeding rate, it was important to continually breed them to maintain numbers and population genetics.[9] Zoos again played a role even when not breeding, providing housing for the 'surplus' non-breeding animals. At the time of writing, a small population of devils has been released on the disease-free Maria Island off the coast of Tasmania, with plans to eventually reintroduce them to the mainland once the disease can be controlled.

disease to wild populations) and the released animals often fare worse than their wild counterparts. Some captive animals will undergo changes that would make reintroduction difficult, such as modifications in the

Figure 4.1: A Tasmanian devil with advanced Devil Facial Tumour Disease

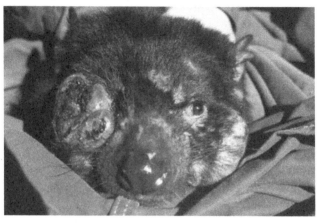

skull morphology of captive lions and tigers that don't have to bring down prey.[10] Most zoo-housed animals never learn the skills required to survive in a wild environment, and training animals for reintroduction requires careful planning. It often means poor welfare for those animals as they are forced to learn to adapt to the harsher conditions of the wild, such as how to find and process food, find shelter and protect themselves from predators. While zoos may aim at preserving natural behaviours in their animals, without additional training this will almost always be insufficient for life in the wild.

Additionally, reintroduction is just not a viable conservation strategy for many species. Reintroduction requires suitable habitat that is not already at carrying capacity (that is, holding the maximum sustainable population) for the species. While some species are threatened by disease or poaching and thus see declines in numbers while habitat remains stable, in most cases it is degradation or loss of habitat that causes species decline. Without suitable habitat for release, reintroduction leads nowhere.

Indeed, most breeding that happens in zoos is for the management of the zoo population, not for conservation. This still needs to be carefully planned to maintain population genetics and demographics for viable long-term populations. Most zoos participate in coordinated regional and global 'studbook' programmes, such as the Association of Zoos and Aquariums' 'Species Survival Plans', that carefully analyse existing populations and make breeding recommendations. But there should not be a false impression that this has a direct conservation benefit, as this is typically only for maintaining existing zoo populations.

If breeding and release were the only means by which zoos could help conserve animals, critics would probably be right that they are not doing well enough to justify their continuation. However, there is also a range of ways zoos can indirectly support conservation, both through assisting in situ conservation and through inspiring behaviour change in their visitors and the wider community.

In situ conservation

Zoo critics are often sceptical of the conservation role of zoos, seeing it as a 'false alibi'.[11] That is, they think zoos present themselves as conservation organizations in order for staff to feel better about the ways they wrong the animals they house, and to improve the zoo's reputation with the public. Critics highlight the importance of in situ over ex situ conservation, arguing that if zoos are only performing the latter role, they are overlooking the most important aspect of conservation. However, this dichotomy ignores the important roles zoos play in supporting in situ conservation.

Instead of conducting their own breeding and release programmes, many zoos aim to support existing conservation efforts that are happening on the ground, cooperating with regional non-governmental organizations and conservation organizations, or even starting their own. There are a lot of local and global projects aimed at protecting habitats and species, rewilding previously disturbed habitats, and ameliorating human–wildlife conflicts, often in conjunction with the local community. Zoos can also run education and awareness-raising campaigns to increase support and raise funds for in situ conservation.

Those who are sceptical of the benefits of zoo-based conservation often argue that there is an opportunity cost for these sorts of initiatives. Zoos, they claim, take resources that could otherwise be used to even greater effect if they were to be directly applied to conservation initiatives. Channelling the money through zoos only depletes the funds and 'greenwashes' the operations of the zoo. Here, we challenge this view.

The first issue is the question of where the money comes from. Some may suggest that instead of spending your money visiting a zoo, feeling justified that you are helping conservation, it would be better to donate it straight to your favourite conservation organization. This seems to misunderstand the motivation for spending in the first place. For most people a zoo visit is first and foremost a day out, not a charitable donation. Refraining from visiting the zoo is far more likely to be replaced by a trip to the movies or a waterslide park than an online donation to a conservation charity. The same goes for government funding of public zoos – this money is part of the city or state recreation budget, not its environment budget. Even if it were true that the money would, all things considered, be better used for direct conservation initiatives, this is not where the money would be redirected were zoos to be closed down, and thus is not a serious argument against zoos.

Part of the conservation support from zoos also consists of donating funds. Conservation initiatives are typically expensive, involving a lot of staff time and equipment. Some zoos allocate part of their entry fees to conservation, or the fees paid for additional experiences such as 'up-close' animal encounters, while others run charitable bodies that fundraise explicitly for conservation (Box 4.2). Globally, zoos are the third-largest contributors to conservation, with around $350 million (USD) spent every year.[12] There are similar complaints that this represents only a tiny fraction of the total operating budget of zoos and thus can't be taken as a serious focus of their activities. However, this overlooks the range of other ways that zoos also focus their operations on conservation action.

Box 4.2: Recycling for wildlife

The National Zoo and Aquarium in Canberra, Australia, where Heather worked for many years, runs a conservation team made up of zoo staff and volunteers contributing their free time to raise money for wildlife conservation projects. One of the most successful ongoing fundraising efforts was implemented by Sue, a dedicated long-time zoo volunteer who would visit the zoo daily to collect plastic containers from the zoo's recycling bins and take them out to the local container deposit site, which offered a 10-cent refund for each container. She now has a volunteer team to assist her and has raised over $40,000 (AUD) for a variety of wildlife charities.

Zoos have another resource that can be of use to conservation projects: expert staff with skills in animal husbandry, veterinary medicine and public relations. All of these can be of great benefit to small conservation organizations, and many zoos regularly 'donate' staff to help out where needed or train colleagues in the developing world. Some zoos have collaborated with local communities in areas of conservation interest (either at home or abroad) in designing and implementing conservation projects that will have meaningful local benefits for both humans and the environment and ongoing engagement from community members. As we saw in the previous chapter, zoos can also contribute to research into endangered species and preservation techniques used in field research.

Probably most importantly, zoos run conservation education and behaviour change campaigns targeted at informing visitors about biodiversity and conservation and encouraging behaviours that benefit animals and the environment. Conservation, at its core, is primarily about human behaviour change; the World Zoo and Aquarium Conservation Strategy lists behaviour change as one of the key components of zoo conservation. It is human actions that have caused the current biodiversity crisis, and it is only through changing human behaviour that lasting conservation initiatives will succeed. Preserving biodiversity means transforming how humans view the natural world, which includes care for wildlife and motivation for environmentally conscious behaviour. Zoos can play this role in a way that arguably no other organization can, through fostering a sense of connection with other animals and inspiring people to act to help animals and the environment. This means that zoos are likely to have the most impact when focused on using their resources to influence the humans that visit or interact with them, which we will examine further in Chapter 5.

Competing values

One of the big challenges in conservation is balancing the values of species and biodiversity preservation against the welfare of individual animals. The values inherent in conservation are aligned with the 'land ethic' advocated by the American wildlife ecologist Aldo Leopold, who claimed that 'a thing is right when it tends to preserve the integrity, stability, and beauty of the biotic community', and 'wrong when it tends to otherwise'.[13] Here, the preservation of ecological communities and their functioning is what takes precedent. Biodiversity and ecosystem functioning are seen to be intrinsically valuable, independent of their effects on any human or other creature. By contrast, an animal welfare ethic is concerned with preventing or minimizing harms to the welfare of individual animals.

Some movements, such as Compassionate Conservation[14] or Conservation Welfare,[15] aim to reduce the conflict between these values by finding ways to align both species value and individual animal interests. This is tied to a recognition that individuals and their wellbeing are not independent of, but instead closely intertwined with, the health and functioning of ecosystems. However, often these operate by limiting the scope of available actions for conservation to those which do not harm individuals. This can therefore be seen as a constraint on conservation activities, rather than complementary to them. While some initiatives may be favoured by both approaches (such as protecting endangered habitat from clearing), others (such as culling invasive species) will be viewed differently. This will also be the case with some zoo activities – for instance, use of 'ambassador' animals, culling 'surplus' individuals or training animals for release – where some harm to welfare may occur. In these cases, the question of which values to prioritize becomes relevant.

Our view is that, in the case of zoos, individual animal welfare should be the priority. Some zoos already adopt this approach – for instance, Jenny Gray (Chief Executive Officer of Zoos Victoria) in her book *Zoo Ethics* concludes that zoo conservation efforts are only ethically defensible when they align with individual animal interests.[16] While conservation goals are important, they should not be pursued at the cost of the individual animals housed in zoos. Unlike conservation efforts in the wild, the activities of zoos risk harm to the animals they hold captive – animals for which they have assumed a responsibility of care. Some views in animal ethics highlight the importance of caring relationships between humans and animals in guiding the scope of our duties towards them.[17] In bringing animals into captivity (either through capture or, much more commonly, through breeding), we assume responsibilities for their care and wellbeing that should outweigh other goals. Our central argument in this book is that zoos are for animals, and as such need to prioritize animal welfare when other goals come into conflict.

We have explored a range of conservation initiatives that zoos can participate in that should not cause any harm to welfare, and it is here that zoos should focus. Of course, there still remains the open question of whether zoos harm animals by their very existence – whether keeping animals captive is itself always a harm. A common narrative about zoos is that the captive animals are in some sense ambassadors or representatives standing in for their wild relatives, suffering a necessary sacrifice (in the form of captivity) for the good of the whole. Even those working in zoos often take this position, making statements such as this one: 'This is the whole paradox of working in a zoo. We know that ideally animals shouldn't be in cages. In an ideal world, we don't exist.'[18] We don't believe this is always true. While some animals may be harmed by some forms of captivity, this is not a necessary feature of zoo animal housing and husbandry, and therefore zoos can undertake their conservation mission without feeling this must always conflict with animal welfare goals.

Conclusion

The strongest justification we have discussed so far for the existence of modern zoos is their role in conservation, helping to protect endangered species and habitats. This is a benefit for the wild animal populations that are preserved, as well as humans and other animals who rely on functioning ecosystems for their survival and flourishing. As with zoos' other roles, the contribution that each one makes to conservation will vary, and some may pay only lip service to conservation aims by virtue of holding endangered species in their collection. However, all accredited institutions should be making some real contribution of the kinds we have covered here – whether through direct conservation breeding, or indirect means such as the donation of funds, or awareness-raising and behaviour change campaigns. Indeed, we have argued that direct contributions to conservation are probably less important than indirect contributions, achieved through supporting in situ conservation projects and inspiring people to care more about the natural world through making connections with animals. However, where conservation aims come into conflict with the welfare of individual animals, zoos have a special responsibility to put their animals first and should focus on conservation goals that align with protecting animal welfare.

5
EDUCATION: TEACHING THROUGH CONNECTION

The fourth traditional pillar for zoos is education. For many zoo visitors – particularly parents planning a family visit – one important goal is to learn more about other animals and the natural world. Zoos have long viewed the fascination and joy that visitors derive from seeing animals as a great opportunity to educate and inspire. This also aligns with the conservation goal, as one of the most powerful ways zoos can achieve their conservation aims is through educating people about endangered animals and how they could be saved, and motivating positive behaviour change to help animals and the environment. However, there is a tension between zoos' claimed educational role and their critics' sceptical assessment of it, which we will explore in this chapter. As with the previous pillars, we will critically examine the educational role of zoos – both historical and current

– and evaluate whether this role can serve to justify zoos' existence.

History of education in zoos

Quite early in their history, zoos became centres of education; a place to see and learn about animals. However, for a long time educational content was minimal, primarily consisting of exhibit signs listing the species name alongside basic facts, such as their distribution and ecology. Some smaller, non-accredited zoos still don't even display this type of basic signage for all their enclosures.

Today, zoos are making an effort to expand the content and approaches used in their education programmes. Most modern zoos have daily keeper presentations, where staff feed and talk about the animals. Many run tours that cover a range of animals and raise environmental issues along the way. Guided tours have been found to increase a feeling of connection to nature and improve attitudes towards species conservation.[1] In large part this is because such talks don't just involve listing biological facts, but also include stories that engage listeners and help them relate to the animals.

There is also an increasing focus on children's education. Many zoos provide specialized tours and interactive experiences aimed at school groups of different ages to supplement their school curricula. Arguably, impact on children is where most of the value of zoo education will lie, as it is through shaping the knowledge, values and actions of a new generation that real change can be realized.

Zoo design can be undertaken to create an immersive educational space, where the visitor feels they are present in the natural habitat of the animal, rather than a zoo. The architect Jon Coe is famous for his work with zoos, applying an understanding of human behaviour to creating spaces that predispose visitors to an enjoyable learning experience where they also subconsciously take in the key messages intended by the institution. He argues that the creation of naturalistic landscapes where visitors can encounter animals through unexpected viewing locations, such as rounding a corner shielded by thick bamboo to find a small window into a tiger habitat, can create a more realistic sense of immersion in the natural world than a series of obvious cages or exhibits lined up in a row.[2]

Many large zoos now have themed regional spaces, housing animals from the same part of the world in an area designed to mimic the architecture and natural features of the region (Figure 5.1). Here, the architecture of the visitor spaces and the enclosures are themselves educational, implicitly conveying information about the species and the local culture. Visitors seem to prefer such exhibits and are more likely to engage with informational displays within immersive spaces as compared to more traditional exhibits.[3] This is echoed by a shift in zoo planning from displays focusing on taxonomic groupings (for example, primates and carnivores) to geographic and ecosystem groupings (for example, Amazon rainforest) that can

Figure 5.1: The entrance to the immersive Amazon and Beyond space at Zoo Miami

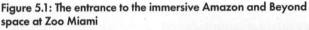

Figure 5.1: The entrance to the immersive Amazon and Beyond space at Zoo Miami

help demonstrate to visitors the interconnectedness between species within their shared environments.

Interactive displays are also becoming common. Visitors can visit 'touch tables' containing a range of interactive animal artefacts such as bones, eggs and feathers, use visual models to compare the sizes of different penguins (and themselves) or scan through a model store to find the products that contain palm oil, the cultivation of which is greatly damaging to many natural habitats. The focus is on games and activities that visitors can engage in to learn more about the species and the threats facing them. Increasingly, such displays make use of technologies such as videos and touchscreens. Research into the effectiveness of more interactive forms of interpretation has found they attract significantly more visitors and hold their attention for longer than standard text and graphics signage.[4]

Zoos can also educate visitors on their own activities as an institution, such as conservation initiatives and research projects they undertake, which are often otherwise hidden from public view. Indeed, educating visitors about conservation efforts is doubly important because here the goal not only becomes to provide visitors with knowledge, but also to encourage changes in their behaviour that can help the natural world.

Behaviour change

Alongside simply passing on knowledge about animals and conservation, zoos also have a role to play in informing about and inspiring behaviour change – to encourage people to care more about the natural world and the problems facing it, and to motivate action. For example, Zoos Victoria implements a 'connect-understand-act' strategy as a tool for behaviour change, based on connecting people with animals, helping them to understand the challenges facing wild populations and inspiring them to conservation action.[5] A great example of a widespread and successful awareness-raising and behaviour change campaign run by zoos across the world is one related to use of sustainable palm oil.

Palm oil is the world's most-used vegetable oil and can be found in a wide range of products, from biofuel to shampoo to chocolate. It is often grown in large monoculture plantations in Southeast Asia, involving clearing local rainforests and ongoing conflicts with wildlife. Palm oil plantations are the major cause of deforestation and wildlife population declines in countries such as Sumatra and Borneo (Figure 5.2). Cultivating sustainable palm oil aims to promote more ecologically friendly methods (for example, using land that has already been cleared and implementing peaceful ways of coexisting with wildlife), but in large part relies on consumer demand to drive uptake. As some of the species most affected, such as orangutans and sun bears, are popular zoo species, zoos have been well-placed to lead such campaigns. This appears to

Figure 5.2: A fragment of rainforest remains among an expanse of palm oil plantations in Sabah, Malaysian Borneo

be most effective when it goes beyond just educational signage and activities. Research has found that when visitors interact with a member of zoo staff who can educate them on the environmental issues surrounding palm oil growth, they will learn more about the topic and are more likely to decide to purchase sustainable palm oil in future.[6]

Awareness-raising campaigns like these can also go beyond the zoo walls and involve the wider community, with zoos leveraging their expertise and reputation to engage the public. Zoos Victoria ran the 'Don't Palm Us Off' campaign that aimed to change Australian labelling laws to require labelling of palm oil on products containing it, which has to date collected almost 500,000 signatures.[7] Chester Zoo in the UK launched a local sustainable palm oil campaign that even resulted in Chester becoming the world's first 'sustainable palm oil' city.[8] The World Association of Zoos and Aquariums created a palm oil scanning app that allows consumers to scan product barcodes and find out which companies have committed to using sustainable palm oil.[9]

One key part of successful campaigns is to provide a clear message about a relevant action zoo visitors can take when they want to help. It's too easy to become overwhelmed by a general need to 'save the planet', but a specific request can be easier to take on board. Visitors asked to do something such as signing a pledge card to keep their cats indoors at night to protect wildlife are more likely to transform conservation intention into action.[10] Zoo conservation messaging should inspire people to feel that they can be part of the solution, rather than overwhelm them with a sense of hopelessness in the face of such large-scale problems. Importantly, efforts of this type should be underwritten by the best available theories of human behaviour change and followed up wherever possible with research to confirm their usefulness. This may be particularly relevant for children, who often feel less empowered than adults to take effective actions.

Fostering a sense of empathy with animals may be the most powerful conservation tool zoos can deploy. Zoos have a unique role in raising awareness and motivating behaviour change because they can link people directly with animals (Box 5.1). The connections that visitors form with the animals they encounter at the zoo can help to inspire action on behalf of the environment and its inhabitants. Not only can they learn what is at stake, but they can come to care enough to change. Visitors who experience animals, particularly during up-close encounters, will have a more positive emotional reaction, feel a closer bond and stronger empathy, recall more information and form greater intentions to perform conservation actions.[11] In particular, a sense of 'empathic concern' that motivates people to want to help other animals[12] can lead to changes in behaviour when accompanied by education regarding what to change.

It is crucial that zoos conduct research to ensure their behaviour change initiatives are having the desired results. Although early efforts relied on a background presumption that positive experiences with wildlife

Box 5.1: Meeting Simbu

Heather used to run zoo animal encounters where visitors were able to have an up-close meeting with a variety of animals. One popular encounter involved meeting Simbu, a Goodfellow's tree-kangaroo living at the National Zoo and Aquarium. Visitors would enter his enclosure and Simbu would come out onto a perch to meet them at eye level, where they could feed him his favourite food – avocado. If he was in the mood for it, they could even stroke his golden-coloured back. Almost everyone left expressing a strong desire to help protect his species, through actions like purchasing fair trade coffee grown by villagers in Papua New Guinea (one of the places tree-kangaroos are found). Watching their sense of wonder at Simbu's closeness, the softness of his fur and the gentle grip of his big claws on the food, and hearing them convey the love he inspired in them, it was obvious how powerful these connections can be.

would be sufficient to create motivation and behaviour change, it is now accepted that this needs to be justified with appropriate evidence. Most often, zoo visitors can only be surveyed about their intentions, or their participation in zoo-site initiatives (such as signing a pledge, donating money or sending a postcard), which may not translate to behaviour change outside the zoo. Some zoos are now investigating this themselves, and there is a growing push within regional and international zoo organizations for their members to measure the effectiveness of their behaviour change programmes. Social scientists can look at the effects on visitors, through interviews and surveys, to determine the changes in beliefs and intentions to change behaviour, or enquiry into follow-up actions. This requires both evaluating the level of connection and caring elicited by the zoo visit, and how this translates to pro-conservation behaviours.

A common finding is that zoo education efforts are more likely to reinforce and motivate existing conservation knowledge and desire for action. This is because zoo visitors tend to already be quite interested in animals and the environment. The upshot of this is that zoos are probably best placed to focus on increasing existing motivation in their visitors, rather than creating a significant change in attitudes. Through creating connections with animals they can increase empathy and motivation to act and can also facilitate action by pointing visitors towards specific behaviours they can adopt.

Criticisms of zoo education

The primary criticism of zoos' educational efforts is that the majority of visitors don't actually engage with them. Most learning experiences at the zoo are informal and voluntary and require capturing and holding attention in order to be successful. Many visitors hardly glance at much of the signage; they are more likely to watch the animals than read about them. Only a small percentage of visitors will stop and engage with any form of interpretation, even the more interactive ones.[13] As we've seen, most visitors to the zoo are there to enjoy themselves rather than to learn something, and will not make an effort to engage with the learning materials even when they are available.

These criticisms should be taken seriously. If visitors are not often engaging with the information and activities provided, the educational role of the zoo is diminished. If, as we have argued, a large part of the goal of education is linked to conservation, then if zoos are failing to educate, they may also be failing to meet their conservation aims. There is a crucial role here for assessment and evaluation of education initiatives, for zoos to make sure that what they are trying is working.

Current research into the effectiveness of zoo education is typically narrow and limited to the specific context of the institution and species studied. Only 15 per cent of zoos report using formal evaluations to assess the effectiveness of their educational materials.[14] Where these have been conducted, there have been some positive results showing that many visitors do come to the zoo intending to learn and that there are long-lasting improvements in biodiversity knowledge following a zoo visit.[15] Overall trends seem to suggest that education is most successful with visitors who already have a broadly pro-environmental mindset, when the visit is longer and when the setting is naturalistic, the animals active and/or some form of connection with the animal is made (even just eye contact).[16]

However, critics are right to note that there are few comprehensive studies and currently the balance of evidence remains quite weak.[17] Even where statistically significant effects are found, these are often small. Most studies are observational only, considering the effect of a single educational condition such as a sign or a keeper talk, without a comparison of different interventions. Changes in knowledge and behaviour can depend on context and background experience, are difficult to assess and the self-reporting methods most commonly used are subject to bias. Making use of alternative methods, such as qualitative analysis, could shed more light. One recent study has proposed using different quantitative and qualitative methodologies to see if they produce the same results, which means the results from each can be used to check and substantiate the other.[18] It is important that zoos continue to evaluate their education initiatives to ensure they are effective and redevelop them when they are not.

Alternatives to zoo education

Alongside the typical criticisms of zoos often lies the proposal that there are alternatives that can do the job at least as well. Ethicist Dale Jamieson raises this very question:

> To what degree does education require keeping wild animals in captivity? Couldn't most of the educational benefits of zoos be obtained by presenting films, slides, lectures and so forth? Indeed, couldn't most of the important education objectives be achieved by exhibiting empty cages with explanations of why they are empty?[19]

After all, research into the effectiveness of forms of media such as videos or webcams has shown that they can also be successful in increasing knowledge and intentions to get involved in conservation.[20]

We have myriad wildlife documentaries that show us the behaviour and ecology of animals as they live in the wild and not just within a captive environment. Whereas at a zoo you are most likely to only see a snow leopard sleeping, a documentary such as *The Frozen Kingdom of the Snow Leopard* allows you to watch them hunt, feed and raise young. There are seemingly more opportunities to craft an educational narrative. And there is no doubt that people enjoy watching animals on screen, as the popularity of wildlife documentaries attests. However, one must keep in mind that documentaries consist of highly selected materials that do not always accurately represent the normal lives of animals. This is part of the reason why zoo visitors are often disappointed to find how much time animals actually spend sleeping, rather than active. Documentaries are not necessarily a more natural alternative. Additionally, these alternatives lack the connection and co-presence we discussed in Chapter 2, which could be a crucial ground for learning and motivation in the zoo.

This does not mean that zoos are better than these alternatives, but rather that both have different (and, we think, complementary) roles to play, focusing on the strengths and weaknesses of each medium. Indeed, there are some creative uses of technology within zoo education. For instance, visitors have reported enjoying a virtual reality behind-the-scenes penguin experience in which they can observe a keeper preparing food and feeding the penguins, as an accompaniment to the experience of seeing the live animals.[21] It may also serve as a useful substitute for up-close animal encounters for the large number of visitors who will not participate in such programmes, or for species that do not enjoy visitor contact. Recently, Twycross Zoo in the UK developed an exhibit featuring holograms of animals, not to replace the experience of the real animals, but to drive home the point that without proper conservation, this will be the only way people may see them in the future.[22]

Another suggestion is that similar connections could be built through wildlife tourism. Seeing animals in the wild creates a sense of wonder and connection alongside an appreciation for the animal within its natural habitat. While we definitely agree that opportunities to view animals in their wild habitats can have a strong and lasting effect – something our own experiences have shown us – this is not a realistic alternative to seeing animals in a zoo. Wildlife tourism can be expensive and will not be available to many people with lower incomes. Additionally, wild spaces are fragile and can only support a small number of wildlife tourists at any time. The 700 million annual zoo visitors could not simply be exported to wild spaces. While wildlife tourism can be very valuable for educational purposes, it cannot be a replacement for zoo visits.

Conclusion

Education is one of the key pillars of zoos, and closely linked to the conservation role. Zoos provide a unique function in connecting people with animals, helping them learn, raising awareness about the problems facing the natural world and motivating changes in behaviour that can help. This cannot simply be replaced by alternative forms of education outside the zoo. The provision of basic education is valuable to all humans. However, if we take the educational role to be closely tied to the conservation role, this is then beneficial to the wild animals assisted and also provides strong justification for the existence of zoos. However, just sticking up signs isn't enough. Careful design is needed to encourage visitors to engage with the educational materials provided, in a way that is fun and memorable. Follow-up research is also needed to ensure that education and behaviour change campaigns are having their desired effects. Without this, critics are right to retain some scepticism about the educational claims made by zoos. However, we are optimistic about the potential for zoos to realize this role in a valuable and meaningful way.

6

ANIMAL WELFARE: THE FIFTH PILLAR

The discussion in the previous chapters has looked at how well the standard goals of zoos – recreation, research, conservation and education – work to justify their existence. However, this type of discussion takes place against an implicit background assumption that zoos *require* justification. The assumption comes from the common belief that animals are worse off for being in captivity, that they would be better off in the wild – what Dale Jamieson refers to as the 'moral presumption against keeping animals in captivity',[1] which he takes to place the burden of proof on those who would keep them. Here we want to challenge this assumption and show that it is entirely possible for zoo animals to have good lives, which should dissolve the requirement for a justification. We argue that animal welfare should be seen as the fifth goal or 'pillar' of the modern zoo. But rather than a mere addition to the other four, we think this should be the primary goal of zoos to ensure that they are for the animals, and not only for humans.

What is good welfare?

Rather than begin this chapter with an investigation of the history of welfare in zoos, we first need to be clear on what we mean by good welfare. Without an understanding of what it means for animals to have sufficiently good welfare, we cannot judge whether zoo animals have good enough lives to justify being housed in captivity. This requires us to answer both the question of what animal welfare is, and what counts as good enough, before moving on to examine whether zoos can provide this standard.

The first question to consider is what we mean by animal welfare. There are four main competing and overlapping views of what animal welfare is: animal feelings, biological functioning, preference satisfaction and natural living. Beginning with the concept of welfare we endorse, the animal feelings view of welfare defines it in terms of the felt experiences of animals. These are often roughly described as pleasures and pains, but really include a diversity of states that feel good or bad for animals, such as hunger, fear, boredom, curiosity, comfort and joy. Under this view, an animal has good welfare when it has mostly positive feelings, and poor welfare when they are mostly negative. This view is popular as it captures the ethical importance of welfare with a focus on the pleasure and suffering animals experience throughout their lives. Though animal feelings are subjective internal states that can be difficult to investigate scientifically, this welfare concept is increasingly common within animal welfare science. This follows the gradual demise of the behaviourist tradition of the mid-20th century, which tried to remove all talk of mental states from science and limit enquiry only to empirically observable phenomena. Animal feelings are now widely seen as valid objects of scientific enquiry.

The second concept of welfare is the biological functioning view. This defines welfare in terms of the animal's physical functioning (that is, good health and fitness). This view was historically popular largely due to the prevalence of behaviourism, and because of animal welfare science's origins in veterinary science. However, this view fails to include forms of psychological suffering most people take to be important for welfare. For this reason, it is typically not used alone but in combination with definitions of welfare that also include other components. Biological functioning is obviously important for welfare – a sick or injured animal will clearly have poor welfare. However, its importance can be captured by the feelings definition of welfare through taking account of the unpleasant feelings these states create in an animal.

The third concept of welfare defines a good life in terms of the satisfaction of preferences. That is, an animal has good welfare when it has its preferences satisfied, and poor welfare when those preferences are frustrated. The main advocate of this view has been

Marian Stamp Dawkins, who takes a 'Two Questions' approach to welfare, asking: Is the animal healthy? And: Does the animal have what it wants?[2] This view raises worries about whether animals' choices can ever be well-informed enough to ground welfare – after all, many animals, if given the choice, would spend their lives gorging on their species' equivalent of junk food. The addition of health to the framework tries to offset this worry, but we still wonder whether animals will always do well in choosing what is good for them – after all, humans often fail in this regard! Additionally, there is still the question of why satisfying preferences holds ethical importance. If it is just because animals feel good when their preferences are satisfied and bad when they are not, then this becomes a version of the animal feelings view. Animal preferences can serve as an excellent guide for what is good or bad for their welfare, but should not be taken unreflectively and instead considered through the lens of how the animal will ultimately feel if the preference is satisfied.

The fourth concept of welfare is natural living. Here, the welfare of an animal is taken to rest in its 'flourishing' in a way that is in line with how its species has evolved, with a focus on performance of normal species-typical behaviours. While this view of welfare has intuitive appeal, it has been criticized primarily because it's difficult to identify what it is about 'naturalness' that really matters.[3] An animal being chased by a predator or starving to death during a drought may be completely natural, but still have poor welfare. And humans have happily given up much of their own naturalness for increases in wellbeing. Natural living may therefore be an important instrumental component of welfare – because many natural behaviours feel good for animals and their frustration feels bad – but not itself what grounds good or poor welfare.

Each of the different accounts of welfare has its own benefits and drawbacks. In practice, they will often align when making recommendations about what living conditions are good or bad for animals. For example, environments that prevent species-typical behaviours are also likely to frustrate preferences and make animals feel bad. In some cases a pluralistic stance – applying different views for different contexts – can be helpful,[4] but ultimately when there are conflicts between these views a choice needs to be made about what to prioritize. We endorse the animal feelings view in these cases as it holds the strongest ethical weight with its focus on prevention of animal suffering. While it may be more difficult to measure, it does a better job at capturing what we – and most importantly, what the animals – care about.

The second question regarding what counts as good welfare is where we set the threshold for what is good enough. We want to determine when and whether zoo animals have sufficiently high welfare to consider their lives in the zoo as worthwhile, such that they don't need additional justification to be kept there. How do we decide what should count as a good enough life? Welfare can be thought of as a spectrum, with poor states of welfare on one end, and good welfare on the other, with some threshold along this line that will count as sufficiently good welfare for a chosen purpose. We will briefly cover four possible thresholds: a neutral line, optimal welfare, the level of welfare of wild animals, and the level of contentment (Figure 6.1).

Figure 6.1: Four possible thresholds for determining what counts as good welfare for zoo animals

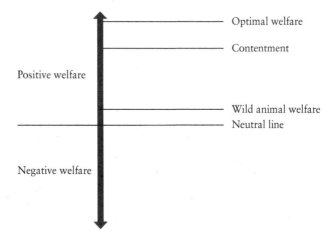

The neutral line for welfare occurs where an animal has more positive than negative experiences, so that their pleasure outweighs their suffering. This might seem like a natural threshold for what counts as sufficiently good welfare, in line with a recent emphasis on positive animal welfare. Indeed, some zoo welfare assessment schemes require that animals are free from negative experiences and have at least one ongoing opportunity for positive experience (see Box 6.2), which appears to implicitly endorse this threshold. The worry here is that this line is too low – that lives just barely above this line aren't really good enough for our purposes. The animals are not suffering, but neither are they really thriving.

On the other end of the scale is the high threshold of optimal welfare. That is, the highest level of welfare the animal can experience. A view like this may underlie claims that any amount of deprivation for zoo animals means they aren't doing well enough to justify their captivity. It should be clear though that this high threshold will never be achievable in practice, as there are resource limitations and necessary trade-offs between positive and negative experiences. Additionally, holding this standard makes it difficult to distinguish adequate and inadequate welfare levels below the threshold. This may best be thought of as an aspirational threshold, one to which all should aspire and that will encourage best practice, even with the acknowledgement that it will never be reached. However, it is too demanding to set as a threshold for the acceptability of housing animals in zoos.

The level of wild animal welfare is an intuitive threshold apparently implicitly held by many who worry about the welfare harms of keeping animals in zoos. Here, the idea is that the lives of zoo animals are only good enough if they are at least as good as their wild relatives. This may be motivated by thoughts that this is in some sense the life these animals are being 'denied' through being kept captive. Although this is not strictly true in most cases, as zoo animals are primarily bred in captivity and would never otherwise have come into existence, there is some sense in which we can understand that close counterparts of this animal could have had a wild existence to which we can compare their welfare. The biggest problem with using this threshold is an empirical one – we just don't know the welfare levels of wild animals, and there is still a lot of disagreement about how good or bad they are. Animals in the wild do have many positive experiences, including some that may be difficult to replicate in a zoo environment, such as behavioural freedom and opportunities for agency. However, they also experience many negative states that they may be protected from in captivity, such as starvation, disease, exposure and predation. It is not immediately obvious that a good life in captivity is worse than life in the wild. Without knowing the quality of wild animal lives, it is difficult to justify using their welfare as a meaningful threshold against which to judge zoo animal welfare. If it turns out, for instance, that life in the wild is pretty bad for many or most animals, this should not licence zoos to lower their standards.

The final threshold is the level of contentment. Here, we can think of welfare as being good enough when the animal is content with how well its life is going. This could be seen as the level at which they are no longer strongly motivated to improve their own condition. Here, we let the animal tell us how they feel about their own welfare state. Where an animal would be content to no longer work hard to improve their own life, this suggests there are no strong reasons for those housing them to push for further improvements – these may be desirable, but not required. Of course, there are then empirical questions around how we determine when an animal has reached this state (for example, through the use of preference and motivation testing to look at how hard the animals will work for improvements, and when this levels off), but it at least seems to be a compelling theoretical threshold and goal to strive towards for zoos. We want animals to not only have a happy life, but one with which they are content. With this in mind, we can turn to examining what zoos are doing to improve the lives of the animals in their care, and what they can do better.

What do zoos do for welfare?

We have established that an animal should be considered to have good welfare when it has what it needs for a happy and content life. In considering the quality of zoo animal welfare we then need to ask: how well do zoos meet this standard? Alongside this, what are zoos doing to ensure the welfare of the animals in their care and how could they be doing better? There has certainly been an evolution in the prevailing ideas about good zoo animal housing and husbandry over the past decades. While there have previously been well-founded concerns about the health and longevity of zoo animals, research into improving husbandry conditions has meant that most animals in zoos now lead longer and healthier lives than ever before and often better than their wild counterparts, with higher survival rates for their young.[5]

While zoos of the past used to focus primarily on maintaining good health and long lives, attention is now on ensuring the animals also feel good, using evidence-based good practice and welfare assessment. The majority of a zoo's operating budget (both time and money) is dedicated to animal care, with the daily work of zookeepers in charge of animal husbandry primarily revolving around maintaining and improving the health and welfare of animals in their care. As Heather knows all too well, this often includes early morning starts and exposure to terrible weather conditions, for low wages. Despite this, the jobs are in high demand – truly a labour of love. Zookeepers are there because they genuinely care about their animals, and they will frequently go above and beyond to provide something extra to improve these animals' lives.

While this work primarily involves removing waste and providing food, provision of enrichment and training is increasingly becoming a core part of a zookeeper's job. Environmental and behavioural enrichment arose out of the concern of founding zoo biologist Heini Hediger with 'occupational therapy' to provide zoo animals with substitutes for the activities they may have spent their time on in the wild. This is in line with concerns often raised by zoo critics: that zoo animals live in impoverished conditions that can lead to boredom. Enrichment is used to enhance the environment and routines of captive animals to create variety and cognitive challenge, reduce boredom and encourage a wider range of natural behaviours (Figure 6.2). However, this only works

Figure 6.2: Forage box enrichment

Dingo Jumbany at the National Zoo and Aquarium searching through a forage box for a variety of hidden treats. Boxes like these are an excellent form of enrichment for many species.

when enrichment is incorporated as a core part of animal care.

One concern with animal welfare enrichment programmes is that they are often seen as an extra to the basic husbandry routines a keeper needs to perform – a luxury activity if there is time left at the end of the day, rather than a necessary part of daily care. Research into the reasons enrichment can be neglected by keepers has shown a range of reasons, including lack of time and institutional support.[6] Some zoo management teams are concerned about a negative public reaction to 'unnatural' enrichment items such as cardboard boxes or old tyres, which can place strong constraints on the options available; though research shows that the behaviours elicited by such enrichment lead to an overall positive perception by visitors.[7] Ensuring adequate enrichment for zoo animals therefore requires support from zoo leadership, including additional resources to ensure it is built into core daily husbandry.

The bond with their human caregivers is also a crucial part of the welfare of captive animals (Box 6.1). There is a large body of research on the effects of human–animal relationships across a range of different captive

Box 6.1: Monkeying around

Zookeepers bond with so many of their animals, and some animals will take advantage of these bonds for their own benefit. Heather spent time working with spider monkeys, a cheeky and inquisitive species who were confident with their keepers and quick to avail themselves of the food treats and enrichment items they were brought. The younger monkeys had a favourite game developed with their keepers: when the keeper was holding a rake, the monkeys would use their hands, feet and prehensile tail to hold onto the other end as their human assistant turned in a circle, spinning them through the air until they let go and tumbled onto the grass, only to jump up and grab on again. Interaction with their keepers provided them with a new and pleasurable activity to engage in, one that wouldn't have been possible with only other monkeys to play with.

animal contexts, where positive relationships enhance welfare and negative relationships detract from it, and an emerging body of research on the effects in zoos.[8] In zoos, the quality of the bond has been found to depend on the amount of time spent with the animal (both hours per week and number of years working together), as well as the species, with keepers forming closer bonds to mammals than other taxa. These bonds can improve welfare both through allowing provision of better husbandry from individuals who know the animals well, care about their wellbeing and understand their needs, and through the direct effects of the social relationship such as positive feelings of comfort and safety.

As well as provisions for good welfare, it is important that zoos continually assess animal welfare to ensure they are meeting their goals. Most zoo accreditation programmes now contain a welfare requirement (Box 6.2). For instance, the World Association of Zoos and Aquariums 2023 Animal Welfare Goal lays out the requirement for all national and regional associations to have an approved animal welfare evaluation programme that accredited institutions comply with.[9] This includes the need for all member institutions to have continuous welfare monitoring programmes. Assessment of welfare can be complex and difficult, but there are now a wide range of possible welfare monitoring frameworks and tools available for use in zoos. Institutions that fail to meet the required welfare standards set by national and international associations will lose their accreditation and take a hit to their

Box 6.2: Animal welfare audits

Part of Heather's job as a welfare officer was to oversee the zoo's animal welfare audits for accreditation. These audits involved welfare assessments for a few randomly chosen species (as well as some key species that were assessed in all zoos). The assessments were based on the 'Five Domains' welfare framework,[10] which involves looking at an animal's welfare across four physical domains (nutrition, environment, health and behavioural opportunities) focused through their impact on the fifth domain (the animal's mental state). To pass, the assessment needed to show that there were no unmanaged negative welfare impacts in any domain, and at least one ongoing positive opportunity or experience for the animal. The assessments were a good opportunity to identify and remedy any previously unnoticed welfare problems. Audits are repeated regularly to maintain accreditation, with the intention of increasing minimum standards each time, so what counts as a good zoo is continually improving.

reputation, thus also making it in their commercial interest to improve welfare.

Some of the larger and more progressive zoos also have their own centres for animal welfare, and animal welfare officers on staff (of which Heather used to be one) to conduct welfare audits and advise on improvements. For instance, the Chicago Zoological Society has developed the WelfareTrak programme,[11] the Detroit Zoo runs a Center for Zoo Animal Welfare and Zoos Victoria (an organization that oversees three Australian zoos) has an internal welfare science department. The number of books and research papers on zoo ethics and zoo animal welfare is also steadily increasing (see the Further Reading list for some examples).

Many zoos are undoubtedly making an effort to focus on and improve animal welfare. This requires them to understand the species in their care, implement appropriate housing and enrichment programmes, and conduct ongoing welfare monitoring. There are a range of different methods of assessing zoo animal welfare, each with its own benefits and limitations.[12] This requires zoos to increase their focus at all levels on the welfare of animals, including appropriate staff training and provision of sufficient time and money for animal welfare initiatives and assessment. However, even with all of this, one may still be concerned that animal welfare in zoos will still be poor. Particularly if zoos themselves cause an inescapable harm to animal welfare simply through the fact of captivity, improving zoo standards can never address the central problem.

Do zoos lack something essential?

Although zoos work hard for the welfare of the animals in their care, those concerned with the animals they house might still hold that captive environments essentially lack something necessary for a good life. That is, that animals held in captivity cannot have all they need to flourish. This may be because they will be missing something in captivity that they need for high welfare, or because the very fact of being in captivity itself is a bad thing for them. Views on animal welfare that are concerned with states of the animal other than their happiness may see the focus on subjective wellbeing as too narrow, failing to recognize the other relevant aspects of animal lives that make them rich and individualized. Primarily, this often relates to freedom.

There is an obvious basic sense in which zoo animals are denied their freedom. They are housed in an enclosure, which they are unable to leave. Whether or not this is seen as a problem in itself will depend on underlying ethical commitments. Those more concerned with animal welfare might see this as unproblematic so long as life within the enclosure is good, while those concerned with rights can take the right to liberty as fundamental. One promising approach is to consider it through the lens of interests, asking the question: do animals have an interest in their own freedom? If they do not, not only would it not harm their welfare to be held captive, but they may not even have a right to freedom.[13]

Given what we know about animal psychology and the ability of most animals to conceptualize abstract concepts such as freedom, it seems unlikely that many animals have an intrinsic interest in their own freedom (though highly intelligent animals that are given most attention by zoo critics, such as great apes, cetaceans or elephants, may constitute exceptions). For most animals, the interest will be purely instrumental – freedom is valuable for the opportunities it provides. There is an important and more fundamental sense of freedom that matters here, and that is the freedom to make choices, to act according to one's own wishes. The central question is then whether zoos can accommodate this sort of freedom.

There is a growing focus within animal welfare research on agency, challenge, choice and control as important conditions for welfare. Many experiments have demonstrated the value animals place on their own agency, taking opportunities to control their own environment, such as marmosets choosing to switch lights on or off when given the chance to do so, regardless of the initial light conditions.[14] Conversely, restriction of choice has been shown to be aversive and is the likely cause of abnormal behaviours sometimes observed in captive animals, such as the repetitive behaviours known as stereotypies. Other research has shown that animals will work to obtain their food even where there is 'free' food available; a phenomenon known as *contrafreeloading*.[15] It is likely that there is a biological basis for the desire for choice and control in both humans and other animals, related to motivating action in the face of challenge.[16] Provision of choice and control is rewarding – animals will show positive responses when offered more choices (such as access to different enclosure spaces), even when they do not use the available alternatives.[17] It is becoming increasingly apparent that the ability to exercise agency and have control over one's own environment is valuable to animals, independent of the value of the specific choices offered.

It is certainly difficult for zoos to provide as many opportunities for animals to exercise these capacities as do wild environments. However, good zoos are taking steps to improve the options and opportunities available for captive animals.[18] Building complex enclosures allows animals to make choices about the types of environments they wish to inhabit – up high or down low, in shade or in sun, in view or out of view of the visitors. Carefully designed enclosure furnishings, keeping in mind the natural history of the animal, can provide opportunities for a range of natural behaviours (such as climbing, flying, swimming, digging). Exhibit 'rotations' that move animals between interconnected habitats can also provide novelty and complexity. Overhead walkways passing through the zoo can expand territory and allow the animals to move outside of their usual enclosure space, to choose where they want to sit and what they want to look at, and are popular with animals such as primates and tigers. With sufficiently large and complex enclosures, the daily activity patterns of some captive animals can closely reflect those of their wild relatives. Modern zoo animal training also focuses on assent, which allows the animals the freedom to choose whether or not to participate.

Improvements in technology also increase the range of options available to animals to control their environments through creative application of 'animal-centred technology'.[19] Some enclosure features or experiences can be activated with sensors, so that an elephant that wants a shower, for example, can press a button to activate the water, rather than waiting for a keeper to come and do it at a scheduled time. Similar setups could allow animals to play sounds or videos, that they would like to hear or see. Providing choices like these can lead to some interesting and unexpected results, such as the findings that some primate species prefer 'unnatural' sounds such as traffic, to more natural animal or ecosystem sounds.[20] Interactive games or other technologies, such as use of iPads or motion-sensor games, can give animals the chance to play or experience cognitive challenges and have been successfully used with orangutans.[21] What is important here is that these provide the animals with control over what they do or experience, and when they do it.

It is also important not to overestimate the amount of behavioural freedom wild animals have. While in some sense they are able to do what they want, they are also constrained by the availability of suitable resources (they cannot swim without access to sufficiently deep water, for instance), the requirement to fulfil other urgent bodily needs, and external pressures from the presence of predators or competitors. A well-designed zoo enclosure built with variety and opportunities for control may end up giving animals more freedom of this kind than their wild environments do. Animals within a zoo environment will thus lack some of the behavioural freedoms that their wild counterparts enjoy, but they will also gain some freedoms that wild animals lack (such as freedom from hunger, predation and exposure to severe weather). There is a trade-off here between different conditions that influence welfare where, as zoo biologist Jake Veasey suggests, the ideal point is likely to lie somewhere in the middle.[22]

Perhaps what should guide decision-making is considerations of whether the animal would consent to the situation if they were able. Though it is obviously difficult to make this decision on behalf of another creature, and we should be careful of self-serving bias in this respect, we should also not automatically assume that animals would never consent to life in a zoo environment. Just as we willingly accept all the restrictions on our own liberties that living in a society entails, in order to gain other benefits, so too perhaps other animals may do the same.

Animal ethicists Lori Gruen and Erika Fleury argue for what they call a 'sanctuary ethos', that seeks to extend consideration for captive animals beyond basic welfare needs to a proper respect for their interests and choices.[23] This seems like a fruitful model for zoos moving forwards – to think beyond just the basic care provisions such as adequate health care and nutrition to encompass the range of behavioural opportunities and regard for agency that are a central part of a good life for any animal.

Conclusion

The welfare of zoo animals should be the highest priority; it is here that we find a point of agreement with zoo critics such as Dale Jamieson, who argues that 'if we keep animals in captivity, what we owe them is everything ... we must conform to the highest standards of treatment and respect'.[24] Animals in zoos live in a special relationship to humans, completely dependent on our care for their quality of life, and that creates a special duty to ensure they flourish. In placing welfare as the highest priority, we can ensure that zoo animals have good lives and that zoos need not struggle to justify their existence. Under these conditions, zoos can confidently say that they are there for animals. While a zoo could fall short in offering a great recreational experience, high quality research, or contributions to conservation and education, it is when it fails to care properly for its animals that we are truly concerned.

Good animal welfare can also help zoos in achieving their other aims. The continuing operations of zoos require them to be endorsed (and visited) by the general public, and this endorsement will often depend on the perception that the animals in the zoo have good welfare. This is also true of meeting aims in education and motivating behaviour change – people who feel bad about the animals they see are unlikely to take away anything beyond this message. Finally, good animal welfare can also improve the success of breeding and conservation projects. Stressed or unhealthy animals will typically be less successful breeders and behavioural deprivations can lead to them losing the capacity for natural behaviours that may be important if intended for future release to the wild.

Here we hope to have shown that there is no necessary trade-off between the aims of a zoo and the welfare of the animals it keeps. Animals in zoos can have good lives when the right conditions are met, and thus zoos do not need to 'justify' their existence through creating other benefits in the world. However, this requires that zoos are working hard to ensure they are providing the best possible care in line with current evidence, including a stronger focus on opportunities for agency, choice and control. In the next chapter we will also discuss some of the primary challenges still facing zoos, challenges that modern zoos need to address to ensure that they maintain community support to operate into the future.

7
WHERE NEXT FOR ZOOS?

As we hope to have made clear, there is no single answer to the question of what zoos are for. Throughout their history their goals have changed as they expanded from collections based on the interests of powerful individuals for the mere entertainment of humans towards the inclusion of other more laudable goals such as research, conservation and education. Together with recreation, these goals have formed the four pillars of the modern zoo and are often cited as justifications for their existence. One reasonable answer to the title question of this book could thus be: 'Zoos are for recreation, research, conservation and education.' However, as we have emphasized, we don't think this goes far enough. Instead, we have argued that zoos are – or should be – for animals, first and foremost. Animal welfare should be their primary goal, with the other four pillars subsidiary to this while providing a range of additional benefits to human and nonhuman animals.

Zoos are for animals

In the ongoing debates between the critics and defenders of zoos there has been an unfortunate assumption that animals in zoos must be inherently harmed through the fact of their captivity; made worse off than their wild counterparts. The captive housing of wild animals is seen as an unfortunate but necessary cost for zoos to achieve their other goals. This may include, for instance, the housing and breeding of endangered species for release back to the wild, or to educate the public about the negative impact humans can have on wild species. In this book we have analysed the four traditional pillars and shown how these goals can at least partially justify the existence and operations of zoos. However, primarily we hope to have shown that there is really no need to engage in this calculation of trade-offs at all.

It is simply not true that zoo animals must inherently be worse off than their wild counterparts. If animals in zoos lead happy lives with opportunities for agency, choice and control, then there no longer appears to be any need to ask for a justification of zoos at all. Instead of taking the traditional view that zoos are mainly for humans, we have argued that it is better to think of modern zoos as being for the animals they house, along with the wild animals they can help. We hope to have made a successful case for making animal welfare the fifth – and central – pillar for zoos.

This is not to imply that contemporary zoos are not already moving in this direction. While the focus is still typically centred on the other four pillars (particularly conservation), many zoos worldwide are making animal welfare one of their core priorities. Our aim here has been to amplify this focus, to encourage zoos to move further in making animal welfare their central goal. This is where we think the zoos of the future should be heading.

When thinking about the multiple goals of zoos, these can naturally conflict with one another, without an easy answer for how we should trade them off against each other. Here, animal welfare can provide a central point from which to assess trade-offs and to reorient the activities of zoos from humans towards the animals. Modern zoos can be for animals (both within the collection and in the wild) as well as for humanity. While there are human benefits such as recreation and research, these are secondary to the larger goals that benefit animals through providing conservation assistance for wild animals and high-welfare housing and husbandry for captive animals. These benefits to animals make zoos a worthwhile institution to support, while continuing to advocate for elimination or improvement of parks that fail to meet these standards, such as 'roadside zoos'. While zoo critics are right that sanctuaries are important – particularly in housing rescued wildlife – zoos are still important for their unique roles in research, education and fostering human connection to animals.

Maintaining high welfare standards is also crucial for zoos to meet their other aims, in particular through sustaining a good reputation. The way the general public views the status and activities of zoos will influence their level of support, and this will in turn impact the *social licence* to operate (that is, the social 'permission' granted by the wider community for an institution to continue its operations). Compare here the example of exotic animals in circuses (Figure 7.1). As public concern grew over the treatment and housing of circus animals, these became increasingly unpopular. Animal-based circuses gradually lost their social licence to operate, until they were placed under regulations that now prevent their operations in many parts of the world.

Without a social licence to operate, zoos will not be able to work towards their wider goals. Reputation is influenced by a range of factors, such as the perception and experience of the actions and values of the institution. Therefore, it is important for zoos to ensure

Figure 7.1: Exotic animal performances in circuses have lost their public appeal

that they are publicizing their positive contributions and paying attention to (and attempting to mitigate) negative perceptions. With strong public concern for the welfare of individual animals, and a history of suspicion towards the ability of zoos to provide good lives for the animals in their care, it is important that zoos explicitly and publicly demonstrate their commitment to animal welfare above all else, in order to remain in operation and to achieve their other goals. High animal welfare is not optional for the zoos of the future, if they wish to continue operating as public scrutiny increases.

Areas for improvement

We have suggested in this book that zoos are capable of providing good lives for many animals. This means there is no necessary trade-off between individual and species interests, as is often suggested in discussions around the ethics of zoos. But this does not imply that there is nothing left to do. We don't intend to be overly uncritical or to imply that we think zoos are doing a perfect job. While we have described some of the best activities zoos are undertaking to meet their goals – particularly relating to animal welfare – many zoos still fall short of this standard. There is thus a need for all zoos to translate the *capacity* for providing good welfare into an actual provision, for all species. Here, we will raise some of the key concerns we think need to be addressed to move modern zoos closer to the ideal of centres for animal flourishing.

The first is improved regulation to ensure the worst zoos can no longer operate. We began by laying out the difference between what we have called 'good' zoos, and the much worse small and poorly run operations such as roadside zoos. These zoos do not contribute to the other aims we have covered in this book, and neither do they provide for the welfare of the animals they house. Despite this, in most regions these zoos are able to persist within the law; regulations are primarily concerned with biosecurity or escape risk, rather than quality of life for the animals. Tighter regulations around who is allowed to house and display exotic animals, with a focus on the ability to provide sufficiently well for animal welfare, is a crucial part of ensuring that only good zoos remain.

This is something all zoos need to get behind. Bad zoos can harm good zoos through lowering the reputation and associated social licence of the entire industry. Indeed, it is the poor practices of bad zoos that are often used by critics to cast doubt on all zoos. Good zoos therefore need to distinguish themselves from bad zoos, as well as to be seen to be acting on the problem of bad zoos that neglect animal welfare (for example, through campaigning for regulation and accreditation of all institutions, or providing assistance to lift standards in zoos in developing countries).

The second improvement is thinking hard about the choice of species through strategic collection planning. Some species may not do well in captivity in any zoo, while others may do better or worse depending on the region. Different species have vastly different needs and even once we know what these are, there will be differences in how well zoos are able to provide them. Some species may be difficult or impossible to meet the needs of within a captive environment. Zoos should build their collections around animals they think are likely to thrive within the conditions they can provide. This might mean avoiding large ungulates and carnivores in space-constrained city zoos, or cold-climate animals in zoos located in warmer regions (Figure 7.2).

Research into the welfare of different species held in zoos has identified which tend to do better or worse, as well as some of the ecological and behavioural correlates most predictive of poor welfare outcomes.[1] For instance, wide-ranging carnivores such as wolves

Figure 7.2: Red panda in the snow

Red pandas are a visitor favourite, but these mountain-dwelling animals prefer snow to sun, and can struggle to cool off when temperatures rise.

and polar bears are most likely to do poorly in zoo environments. Parrots with large brains and wild diets that involve complex and time-consuming food handling – such as extracting grubs from trees, or cracking large nuts – similarly do worse in captivity. More generally, some of the predictors of poor welfare include being highly migratory, having a shy temperament and fixed rather than flexible behaviour patterns. Additionally, some more cognitively complex animals – such as great apes, elephants and cetaceans – may have sufficient capacities to be considered self-aware 'persons' who are aware of their own situation and should be given the same rights to freedom as human persons (Box 7.1).

Perhaps most of these more challenging species should not be housed at all, at least until suitable conditions are found to prevent the negative effects. The hope is that research of this type can also help to identify the core aspects of the captive environment that are problematic and amend them accordingly. However, where this is not possible, zoos should take seriously the possibility that these animals are unsuitable for a zoo environment. Zoos are often keen to display the most popular and charismatic species the public have come to expect, and research suggests that zoo visitors do prefer collections containing a larger number of species,[2] meaning that zoos must to some degree trade off welfare and other concerns (for example, raising funds and awareness for conservation initiatives) in collection planning. There is the possibility that by moving away from housing some of the species visitors

Box 7.1: Is an elephant a person?

Happy the elephant has lived at the Bronx Zoo since her capture from Thailand in 1977. She's lived alone since 2005, when her last companion died, although she still has fence contact with another elephant. In 2018, the Nonhuman Rights Project brought forward a case to the New York Supreme Court, asking that Happy be released to a sanctuary. They filed for a writ of habeas corpus, which can be obtained on behalf of a person who has been unlawfully detained. They argued that as elephants are autonomous and cognitively complex individuals, they should be recognized as persons under the law, with the corresponding right to liberty. In response, the Bronx Zoo argued that she is not a captive person, but an elephant who is well cared for in her one-acre enclosure and 'respected as the magnificent creature she is'.[3] The court agreed, ruling against the case on the grounds that habeas corpus is intended only to apply to human beings. However, the vote was split 5-2, indicating that some judges already take this possibility seriously, and it may not be long before we see some form of legal recognition of the personhood of an animal.

most want to see, zoos may experience a decrease in visitor numbers. However, the welfare needs of their animals must come first. Zoos can mitigate negative impact through careful communication with visitors about the welfare considerations that have led to their decision and by trying to find alternative species that are similarly attractive but better-suited to captivity.

With the right housing and presentation, the 'less interesting' species may become just as interesting to zoo visitors. In the words of eminent zoo biologist, the late Terry Maple, the best way forward for zoos is 'fewer animals, living well'.[4]

One further big question about the welfare of zoo animals comes from the potential harm of their death. Zoo animals are frequently euthanized when they are extremely sick or seriously injured. However, these decisions are typically uncontroversial (save for disagreements about when the 'tipping point' is reached where quality of life is no longer worth preserving), as preventing ongoing suffering is considered to be in the interests of the animal. A more complex case comes from the practice of culling so-called 'surplus' animals.

In order to maintain genetically healthy and reproductively viable populations, it is important that zoos continue to breed animals. However, this creates a need for space to house them and resources to care for them, and in the face of these resource and space constraints some zoos have opted instead to cull the animals they don't need for their breeding programmes – a practice that has created some outcry (see Box 7.2). There are welfare considerations on both sides – premature ending of life is a welfare harm in that it deprives an animal of its potential future experiences, but prevention of breeding is a welfare harm to individuals who never get to experience reproductive and parental behaviour.[5] Zoo critics see the practice of culling as representative of the failure of zoos to properly consider the individuality and rights

Box 7.2: Marius the giraffe

In 2014, a young male giraffe named Marius was euthanized at the Copenhagen Zoo. He was not sick or injured, but surplus to the requirements of the zoo's breeding programme. The event raised a public outcry and media frenzy, as many were horrified to see an otherwise healthy animal killed. The zoo defended their actions, noting that Marius had been killed quietly and without suffering and that this was necessary if the zoo wanted to use its resources effectively to maintain a viable breeding population. They also pointed out the value that had been created by his death: the zoo performed a public autopsy for educational purposes, and used some of the meat as food for the carnivores. While it's difficult to know how widespread the practice is, some estimates suggest at least three to five thousand animals a year are similarly culled in zoos across the world.[6]

of the animals they house. Where zoos cull animals, they are placing animals in the role of members of a reproductive population, as opposed to individuals worthy of individual consideration.

In practice, there is no perfect solution for a problem like this – breeding and caring behaviour are undoubtedly sources of positive welfare, and finite resources mean that those used to care for one animal must be redirected from another. However, as we have already noted, zoos have a special duty to the animals in their care that should outweigh conservation aims where these do conflict. With careful breeding management and a commitment to care for offspring as far as possible, zoos can at least minimize the problem, and should pursue alternatives wherever possible. For instance, as 'surplus' animals are more often males, research into how best to introduce males (particularly unrelated individuals) into all-male 'bachelor groups' can help zoos house males in larger single-sex groups rather than culling them. In some limited instances, release to the wild may even be appropriate. What is most important is that a practice like this is not undertaken indiscriminately and zoos do everything within their power to ensure it is used only as a last resort.

Finally, there is the issue of the use of animals as feed.[7] Zoos house many carnivores, and those carnivores eat meat. Therefore, the welfare footprint of a zoo is larger than just that of the animals it houses. The animals that are raised and killed to feed the zoo inhabitants are also worthy of consideration. As most animals killed for meat are raised in intensive farms with poor welfare standards, this means that housing and feeding any carnivore is likely to result in net suffering.

Additionally, many zoos raise their own 'feed' animals, typically the smaller species such as mice and rats (most often fed to reptiles) as well as insects such as crickets or mealworms for the smaller insectivores and omnivores, such as meerkats and small primates. It is still an open question whether insects are sentient, though recent work suggests this possibility should be taken seriously.[8] Mice and rats undoubtedly are. However, these animals are typically given only a fraction of the care that the animals in the main collection receive. Mice and rats can be housed in the same small cages seen in biomedical research, with little space or complexity – something that would be completely unacceptable for a similar rodent species on display at the zoo.

The problem of the welfare of their food animals is therefore one that zoos need to take seriously. At the extreme end, this may suggest that zoos should not house carnivores at all, but perhaps a more moderate view is that zoos should be careful to source humanely raised (not intensively farmed) meat, and ensure they use the same standards of care for their 'feed' animals as they do for their 'display' animals. Ethicist Josh Milburn has also suggested the possible future use of lab-grown meat for carnivore feed,[9] a solution we are optimistic about.

Linked to the issue of the welfare of feed animals is the question of live feeding. Although feeding of live prey can encourage a range of natural behaviours that are probably rewarding for predators to perform, it will also be a source of fear and pain for the prey animals. For this reason, live feeding of vertebrate animals is discouraged or prohibited in most zoos, though there are strong cultural differences regarding the perceived permissibility of the practice.[10] Overcoming such beliefs is an important part of ensuring the welfare of feed animals, who are certain to suffer during live feeding. Careful design of behavioural enrichments – such as use of lures or bungees for feeding – can help stimulate many of the same natural behaviours for the predator.

Live feeding of invertebrates is more common globally, and if the possibility of invertebrate sentience is taken seriously, this practice should also be regulated in the same way as other live feeds.

Conclusion

In this book we have examined the range of activities zoos engage in and hope to have made the case that zoos are for animals, with the suggestion that animal welfare should be the central aim. This is not to say that we think zoos are currently doing an ideal job. After all, a government may exist to represent the interests of its voters, all the while doing a terrible job at that. As we have discussed throughout, there are still many areas for improvement if zoos want to live up to the ideal of doing well for animals. These include the ongoing development of zoo welfare science and improvements in enrichment and enclosure design to maximize animal agency and control in their environments, with the vision of making zoos an overwhelmingly positive place for the animals they choose to keep. In some cases, this may require a significant revision of current practices, including strict regulation or abolition of for-profit zoos, more rigorous assessment of the choice of species to house, and evaluating the practices of killing surplus animals and animals used for food.

Overall, the message we hope to have made clear throughout is that while zoos can in principle be good places for animals, in many cases there will be substantial changes required before this is true in practice. This also applies to the other pillars of recreation, research, conservation and education, all of which constitute important goals for zoos, but can be executed in a better or worse fashion. In this book, we have outlined many of the ways in which zoos can be improved to serve these important roles in our society and, most importantly, to serve the interests of animals.

We hope you have enjoyed this book and will think of our arguments the next time you step into a zoo or aquarium. Can you find anything there that you think could be improved? Talk to the zoo staff about the goals of their institution and how they are pursuing them to find out more about what modern zoos are really doing for humans and other animals. Our hope is that zoos and the public alike can continue to work together towards the goal of making zoos successful centres for animal flourishing.

NOTES

Chapter 1

1   Anne Safiya Clay and Ingrid J. Visseren-Hamakers, 'Individuals
    Matter: Dilemmas and Solutions in Conservation and Animal
    Welfare Practices in Zoos', *Animals* 12, no. 3 (January 2022): 398,
    https://doi.org/10.3390/ani12030398.

2   For example, Dale Jamieson, 'Against Zoos', *Environmental Ethics:
    Readings in Theory and Application* 5 (1985): pp 97–103; Bob
    Mullan and Garry Marvin, *Zoo Culture* (MW Books Ltd, 1987).

3   Clay and Visseren-Hamakers, 'Individuals Matter', p 10.

4   For example, Michael Hutchins, Brandie Smith and Ruth Allard,
    'In Defense of Zoos and Aquariums: The Ethical Basis for Keeping
    Wild Animals in Captivity', *Journal of the American Veterinary
    Medical Association* 223, no. 7 (1 October 2003): pp 958–66,
    https://doi.org/10.2460/javma.2003.223.958-2; Jenny Gray, *Zoo
    Ethics: The Challenges of Compassionate Conservation* (Cornell
    University Press, 2017).

5   https://www.waza.org/members/waza-members/.

6   https://www.aza.org/connect-stories/stories/interesting-zoo-
    aquarium-statistics.

7   Kailer K. Riedman, Gregory B. Cunningham and Louis DiVincenti,
    'Does Accreditation by the Association of Zoos and Aquariums
    Correlate with Animal Welfare Act Compliance?', *Journal of
    Applied Animal Welfare Science* 26, no. 4 (2 October 2023):
    pp 685–92, https://doi.org/10.1080/10888705.2022.2028150.

8   Phillip J. Greenwell, Lisa M. Riley, Ricardo Lemos de Figueiredo,
    James E. Brereton, Andrew Mooney and Paul E. Rose, 'The
    Societal Value of the Modern Zoo: A Commentary on How
    Zoos Can Positively Impact on Human Populations Locally
    and Globally', *Journal of Zoological and Botanical Gardens*
    4, no. 1 (13 January 2023): pp 53–69, https://doi.org/10.3390/
    jzbg4010006.

9   George B. Rabb, 'The Changing Roles of Zoological Parks in Conserving Biological Diversity', *American Zoologist* 34, no. 1 (1 February 1994): pp 159–64, https://doi.org/10.1093/icb/34.1.159.

10 See, for example, Paul E. Rose and Lisa M. Riley, 'Expanding the Role of the Future Zoo: Wellbeing Should Become the Fifth Aim for Modern Zoos', *Frontiers in Psychology* 13 (20 October 2022): 1018722, https://doi.org/10.3389/fpsyg.2022.1018722.

Chapter 2

1   Vernon N. Kisling, ed, *Zoo and Aquarium History: Ancient Animal Collections to Zoological Gardens* (CRC Press, 2001), pp vii–viii.

2   Kisling, *Zoo and Aquarium History*, p viii.

3   Louise S. Reade and Natalie K. Waran, 'The Modern Zoo: How Do People Perceive Zoo Animals?', *Applied Animal Behaviour Science*, 47, no. 1 (1 April 1996): pp 109–18, https://doi.org/10.1016/0168-1591(95)01014-9; David B. Klenosky and Carol D. Saunders, 'Put Me in the Zoo! A Laddering Study of Zoo Visitor Motives', *Tourism Review International* 11, no. 3 (1 December 2007): pp 317–27, https://doi.org/10.3727/154427207783948757.

4   Kisling, *Zoo and Aquarium History*, p 103.

5   Ralph Acampora, 'Zoos and Eyes: Contesting Captivity and Seeking Successor Practices', *Society & Animals* 13, no. 1 (1 January 2005): pp 69–88, at 74, https://doi.org/10.1163/1568530053966643.

6   Skylar L. Muller, Samantha L. Bissell, Kristen M. Cunningham and Rosemary Strasser, 'How Do You Behave at the Zoo? A Look at Visitor Perceptions of Other Visitors' Behavior at the Zoo', *Animal Behavior and Cognition* 8, no. 4 (1 November 2021): pp 619–31, https://doi.org/10.26451/abc.08.04.12.2021.

7   Courtney Collins, Sean McKeown and Ruth O'Riordan, 'A Comprehensive Investigation of Negative Visitor Behaviour in the Zoo Setting and Captive Animals' Behavioural Response', *Heliyon* 9, no. 6 (1 June 2023): e16879, https://doi.org/10.1016/j.heliyon.2023.e16879; Courtney Collins, Yotam Barr, Sean McKeown, Juan Scheun, Claudia Tay and Ruth O'Riordan, 'An International Investigation of the Prevalence of Negative Visitor Behaviour in the Zoo', *Animals* 13, no. 16 (January 2023): 2661, https://doi.org/10.3390/ani13162661.

8   Acampora, 'Zoos and Eyes'; Mullan and Marvin, *Zoo Culture*; Randy Malamud, *Reading Zoos: Representations of Animals and Captivity* (NYU Press, 1998).

9   Clay and Visseren-Hamakers, 'Individuals Matter'.

10 Reviewed in Andrea M. Godinez and Eduardo J. Fernandez, 'What Is the Zoo Experience? How Zoos Impact a Visitor's Behaviors, Perceptions, and Conservation Efforts', *Frontiers in Psychology* 10 (2019), https://www.frontiersin.org/articles/10.3389/fpsyg.2019.01746.

11 Simon Coghlan, 'An Irreducible Understanding of Animal Dignity', *Journal of Social Philosophy* 55, no 1, (24 July 2023), pp 124–42, https://doi.org/10.1111/josp.12543.

12 Peter Singer, 'Speciesism and Moral Status', *Metaphilosophy* 40, no. 3–4 (2009): pp 567–81, https://doi.org/10.1111/j.1467-9973.2009.01608.x.

13 Remy Debes, 'Dignity', in *The Stanford Encyclopedia of Philosophy*, ed Edward N. Zalta and Uri Nodelman, Spring 2023 (Metaphysics Research Lab, Stanford University, 2023), https://plato.stanford.edu/archives/spr2023/entries/dignity/; Ruth Macklin, 'Dignity Is a Useless Concept', *BMJ* 327, no. 7429 (18 December 2003): pp 1419–20, https://doi.org/10.1136/bmj.327.7429.1419.

14 Federico Zuolo, 'Dignity and Animals. Does It Make Sense to Apply the Concept of Dignity to All Sentient Beings?', *Ethical Theory and Moral Practice* 19, no. 5 (1 November 2016): pp 1117–30, https://doi.org/10.1007/s10677-016-9695-8.

15 See reviews in Eduardo J. Fernandez, Michael A. Tamborski, Sarah R. Pickens and William Timberlake, 'Animal–Visitor Interactions in the Modern Zoo: Conflicts and Interventions', *Applied Animal Behaviour Science* 120, no. 1–2 (August 2009): pp 1–8, https://doi.org/10.1016/j.applanim.2009.06.002; Sally L. Sherwen and Paul H. Hemsworth, 'The Visitor Effect on Zoo Animals: Implications and Opportunities for Zoo Animal Welfare', *Animals* 9, no. 6 (June 2019): 366, https://doi.org/10.3390/ani9060366; Ellen Williams, Violet Hunton, Geoff Hosey and Samantha J. Ward, 'The Impact of Visitors on Non-Primate Species in Zoos: A Quantitative Review', *Animals* 13, no. 7 (January 2023): 1178, https://doi.org/10.3390/ani13071178.

16 See reviews in Ellen Williams, Anne Carter, Jessica Rendle and Samantha J. Ward, 'Impacts of COVID-19 on Animals in Zoos: A Longitudinal Multi-Species Analysis', *Journal of Zoological and Botanical Gardens* 2, no. 2 (June 2021): pp 130–45, https://doi.org/

10.3390/jzbg2020010; Ellen Williams, Anne Carter, Jessica Rendle and Samantha J. Ward, 'Understanding Impacts of Zoo Visitors: Quantifying Behavioural Changes of Two Popular Zoo Species during COVID-19 Closures', *Applied Animal Behaviour Science* 236 (1 March 2021): 105253, https://doi.org/10.1016/j.applanim.2021.105253; as well as individual studies: Laura M. Bernstein-Kurtycz, Diana Koester, Rebecca J. Snyder, Jennifer Vonk, Mark A. Willis and Kristen E. Lukas, '"Bearly" Changing with the Seasons: Bears of Five Species Show Few Behavioral Changes Across Seasons and at Varying Visitor Densities', *Animal Behavior and Cognition* 8, no. 4 (1 November 2021): pp 538–57, https://doi.org/10.26451/abc.08.04.07.2021; Megan Jones, Kylen N. Gartland and Grace Fuller, 'Effects of Visitor Presence and Crowd Size on Zoo-Housed Red Kangaroos (Macropus rufus) During and After a COVID-19 Closure', *Animal Behavior and Cognition* 8, no. 4 (1 November 2021): pp 521–37, https://doi.org/10.26451/abc.08.04.06.2021; Primrose Manning, Elisabeth Dawson, Christina Tholander and Maud Bonato, 'The Effect of COVID-19 Lockdown Restrictions on Self-Directed Behaviour, Activity Budgets, Movement Patterns, and Spatial Use in Semi-Captive African Elephants (*Loxodonta africana*)', *Applied Animal Behaviour Science* (20 July 2023): 106007, https://doi.org/10.1016/j.applanim.2023.106007.

[17] Geoff Hosey, Samantha Ward and Vicky Melfi, 'The Effect of Visitors on the Behaviour of Zoo-Housed Primates: A Test of Four Hypotheses', *Applied Animal Behaviour Science* (24 April 2023): 105938, https://doi.org/10.1016/j.applanim.2023.105938; Marina B. Queiroz and Robert J. Young, 'The Different Physical and Behavioural Characteristics of Zoo Mammals That Influence Their Response to Visitors', *Animals* 8, no. 8 (August 2018): 139, https://doi.org/10.3390/ani8080139.

[18] https://taronga.org.au/sites/default/files/content/pdf/Animal_Welfare_Charter.pdf.

[19] *Zoo 2000: A Look Beyond the Bars*, first edition (British Broadcasting Corporation, 1984); Mullan and Marvin, *Zoo Culture*; Kenneth J. Polakowski, 'A Design Approach to Zoological Exhibits: The Zoo as Theater', *Zoo Biology* 8, no. S1 (1989): pp 127–39, https://doi.org/10.1002/zoo.1430080513.

[20] Edward O. Wilson, ed, *Biophilia* (Harvard University Press, 1984).

[21] John Berger, *About Looking* (Pantheon Books, 1980).

22   Coral M. Bruni, John Fraser and P. Wesley Schultz, 'The Value of Zoo Experiences for Connecting People with Nature', *Visitor Studies* 11, no. 2 (20 October 2008): pp 139–50, https://doi.org/10.1080/10645570802355489.

23   Ursula S. Anderson, Angela S. Kelling, Robin Pressley-Keough, Mollie A. Bloomsmith and Terry L. Maple, 'Enhancing the Zoo Visitor's Experience by Public Animal Training and Oral Interpretation at an Otter Exhibit', *Environment and Behavior* 35, no. 6 (1 November 2003): pp 826–41, https://doi.org/10.1177/0013916503254746; Jerry F. Luebke, Jason V. Watters, Jan Packer, Lance J. Miller and David M. Powell, 'Zoo Visitors' Affective Responses to Observing Animal Behaviors', *Visitor Studies* 19, no. 1 (2 January 2016): pp 60–76, https://doi.org/10.1080/10645578.2016.1144028.

24   Juno Salazar Parreñas, *Decolonizing Extinction: The Work of Care in Orangutan Rehabilitation* (Duke University Press, 2018), p 62.

25   Thomas Welsh and Samantha Ward, 'Visitor Attachment to Dolphins during an Interaction Programme, Are There Implications to Dolphin Behavior?', *Zoo Biology* (12 July 2021): zoo.21634, https://doi.org/10.1002/zoo.21634.

26   Lynda Birke, Geoff Hosey and Vicky Melfi, '"You Can't Really Hug a Tiger": Zookeepers and Their Bonds with Animals', *Anthrozoös* (3 September 2019), https://www.tandfonline.com/doi/abs/10.1080/08927936.2019.1645504; Geoff Hosey and Vicky Melfi, "Human–Animal Bonds Between Zoo Professionals and the Animals in Their Care," *Zoo Biology* 31, no. 1 (2012): pp 13–26, https://doi.org/10.1002/zoo.20359; Vicky Melfi, Lindsay Skyner, Lynda Birke, Samantha J. Ward, Wendy S. Shaw and Geoff Hosey, 'Furred and Feathered Friends: How Attached Are Zookeepers to the Animals in Their Care?', *Zoo Biology* 41, no. 2 (2022): pp 122–9, https://doi.org/10.1002/zoo.21656.

27   Reade and Waran, 'The Modern Zoo'.

Chapter 3

1   Heini Hediger, *Man and Animal in the Zoo: Zoo Biology* (Delacorte Press, 1969).

2   Andrew K. Schulz, Cassie Shriver, Catie Aubuchon, Emily G. Weigel, Michelle Kolar, Joseph R. Mendelson III and David L. Hu, 'A Guide for Successful Research Collaborations between Zoos and Universities', *Integrative and Comparative Biology* 62, no. 5 (6 December 2022): pp 1174–85, https://doi.org/10.1093/icb/icac096.

3   https://manyzoos.weebly.com/.

4   EAZA Research Standards, https://www.eaza.net/assets/Uploads/
    EAZA-Documents-2022/2022-04-EAZA-Research-Standards.pdf.

5   https://www.zoosciencelibrary.org/en/.

6   Paul E. Rose, James E. Brereton, Lewis J. Rowden, Ricardo Lemos
    de Figueiredo and Lisa M. Riley, 'What's New from the Zoo? An
    Analysis of Ten Years of Zoo-Themed Research Output', *Palgrave
    Communications* 5, no. 1 (29 October 2019): 128, https://doi.org/
    10.1057/s41599-019-0345-3.

7   Aimee Holland, Elena Giulia Galardi, Martina Fabbroni, Anita
    Hashmi, Jerome Catinaud, Richard Preziosi, James Edward
    Brereton and Giovanni Quintavalle Pastorino, 'Exploration of
    Social Proximity and Behavior in Captive Malayan Tigers and
    Their Cubs', *Animals* 13, no. 6 (January 2023): 1040, https://doi.
    org/10.3390/ani13061040.

8   V.A. Melfi, 'There Are Big Gaps in Our Knowledge, and Thus
    Approach, to Zoo Animal Welfare: A Case for Evidence-Based Zoo
    Animal Management', *Zoo Biology* 28, no. 6 (2009): pp 574–88,
    https://doi.org/10.1002/zoo.20288.

9   Danielle Free and Sarah Wolfensohn, 'Assessing the Welfare
    of Captive Group-Housed Cockroaches, *Gromphadorhina
    oblongonota*', *Animals* 13, no. 21 (27 October 2023): 3351,
    https://doi.org/10.3390/ani13213351.

10 Emma S. McEwen, Elizabeth Warren, Sadie Tenpas, Benjamin
    Jones, Kresimir Durdevic, Emilie Rapport Munro, et al, 'Primate
    Cognition in Zoos: Reviewing the Impact of Zoo-Based Research
    over 15 Years', *American Journal of Primatology* 84, no. 10
    (2022): e23369, https://doi.org/10.1002/ajp.23369.

11 Jordyn Truax, Jennifer Vonk, Joy L. Vincent, and Zebulon Kade
    Bell, 'Teamwork Makes the String Work: A Pilot Test of the Loose
    String Task with African Crested Porcupines (*Hystrix cristata*)',
    Journal of Zoological and Botanical Gardens 3, no. 3 (2022):
    pp 448–62, https://doi.org/10.3390/jzbg3030034.

12 Eszter Mátrai, Suzanne M. Gendron, Michael Boos and Ákos Pogány,
    'Cognitive Group Testing Promotes Affiliative Behaviors in Dolphins',
    Journal of Applied Animal Welfare Science 27, no. 1 (2024):
    pp 165–79, https://doi.org/10.1080/10888705.2022.2149267.

13 Fay E. Clark, 'Bridging Pure Cognitive Research and Cognitive
    Enrichment', *Animal Cognition* (2 June 2022), https://doi.org/
    10.1007/s10071-022-01636-2.

[14]   Terry L. Maple and Sally L. Sherwen, 'Does Research Have a Place in the Zoological Garden?', in *Scientific Foundations of Zoos and Aquariums*, ed Allison B. Kaufman, Meredith J. Bashaw and Terry L. Maple, 1st edn (Cambridge University Press, 2019), pp 618–45, https://doi.org/10.1017/9781108183147.024.

Chapter 4

[1]   Reade and Waran, 'The Modern Zoo'.

[2]   Jamieson, 'Against Zoos'; Dale Jamieson, 'Zoos Revisited', in Bryan G. Norton, Michael Hutchins, Elizabeth F. Stevens and Terry L. Maple, eds, *Ethics on the Ark* (Smithsonian Institution Press, 1995), pp 52–66.

[3]   IUDZG/CBSG (IUCN/SSC), *The World Zoo Conservation Strategy: The Role of the Zoos and Aquaria of the World in Global Conservation* (Chicago Zoological Society, 1993); new editions in 2005 [WAZA, *Building a Future for Wildlife: The World Zoo and Aquarium Conservation Strategy*, ed Peter J.S. Olney (WAZA Executive Office, 2005), https://www.waza.org/wp-content/uploads/2019/03/wzacs-en.pdf] and 2015 [R. Barongi, F.A. Fisken, M. Parker and M. Gusset, eds, *Committing to Conservation: The World Zoo and Aquarium Conservation Strategy* (World Assocation of Zoos and Aquariums, 2015), https://www.waza.org/wp-content/uploads/2019/03/WAZA-Conservation-Strategy-2015_Landscape.pdf].

[4]   Gray, *Zoo Ethics*, p xvi.

[5]   See Andrew Moss, Matea Vukelic, Susan L. Walker, Charlotte Smith and Sarah L. Spooner, 'The Role of Zoos and Aquariums in Contributing to the Kunming–Montreal Global Biodiversity Framework', *Journal of Zoological and Botanical Gardens* 4, no. 2 (June 2023): pp 445–61, https://doi.org/10.3390/jzbg4020033 for an extended discussion of how zoos can contribute to the Framework goals and targets.

[6]   Friederike C. Bolam, Louise Mair, Marco Angelico, Thomas M. Brooks, Mark Burgman, Claudia Hermes, et al, 'How Many Bird and Mammal Extinctions Has Recent Conservation Action Prevented?', *Conservation Letters* 14, no. 1 (2021): e12762, https://doi.org/10.1111/conl.12762.

[7]   Lauren A. Harrington, Axel Moehrenschlager, Merryl Gelling, Rob P.D. Atkinson, Joelene Hughes and David W. Macdonald, 'Conflicting and Complementary Ethics of Animal Welfare Considerations in Reintroductions: Welfare in Reintroductions',

Conservation Biology 27, no. 3 (June 2013): pp 486–500; Benjamin Beck, 'Reintroduction, Zoos, Conservation, and Animal Welfare', in *Ethics on the Ark*, ed Bryan G. Norton, Michael Hutchins, Elizabeth F. Stevens and Terry L. Maple (Smithsonian Institution Press, 1995), pp 155–63.

8   https://nre.tas.gov.au/conservation/threatened-species-and-communities/lists-of-threatened-species/threatened-species-vertebrates/save-the-tasmanian-devil-program/about-dftd.

9   Tamara Keeley, Kiara Ritky and Tracey Russell, 'A Retrospective Examination of Factors Associated with Breeding Success of Tasmanian Devils in Captivity (2006 to 2012)', *Journal of Zoo and Aquarium Research* 11, no. 1 (31 January 2023): pp 211–19, https://doi.org/10.19227/jzar.v11i1.667.

10 David M. Cooper, Nobuyuki Yamaguchi, David W. Macdonald, Bruce D. Patterson, Galina P. Salkina, Viktor G. Yudin, et al, 'Getting to the Meat of It: The Effects of a Captive Diet upon the Skull Morphology of the Lion and Tiger', *Animals* 13, no. 23 (22 November 2023): 3616, https://doi.org/10.3390/ani13233616.

11 Clay and Visseren-Hamakers, 'Individuals Matter', p 13.

12 Markus Gusset and Gerald Dick, 'The Global Reach of Zoos and Aquariums in Visitor Numbers and Conservation Expenditures', *Zoo Biology* 30, no. 5 (2011): pp 566–9, https://doi.org/10.1002/zoo.20369.

13 Aldo Leopold, 'The Land Ethic', in *A Sand County Almanac: And Sketches Here and There* (Oxford University Press, 1949), pp 201–26.

14 Gray, *Zoo Ethics*.

15 Ngaio J. Beausoleil, David J. Mellor, Liv Baker, Sandra E. Baker, Mariagrazia Bellio, Alison S. Clarke, et al, '"Feelings and Fitness" Not "Feelings or Fitness": The *Raison d'être* of Conservation Welfare, Which Aligns Conservation and Animal Welfare Objectives', *Frontiers in Veterinary Science* 5, no. 296 (27 November 2018), https://doi.org/10.3389/fvets.2018.00296.

16 Gray, *Zoo Ethics*.

17 Clare Palmer, *Animal Ethics in Context* (Columbia University Press, 2010); Lori Gruen, *Entangled Empathy: An Alternative Ethic for Our Relationships with Animals* (Lantern Books, 2015).

18 Clay and Visseren-Hamakers, 'Individuals Matter', p 11.

Chapter 5

1   Matthias Winfried Kleespies, Viktoria Feucht, Martin Becker and Paul Wilhelm Dierkes, 'Environmental Education in Zoos:

Exploring the Impact of Guided Zoo Tours on Connection to Nature and Attitudes towards Species Conservation', *Journal of Zoological and Botanical Gardens* 3, no. 1 (March 2022): pp 56–68, https://doi.org/10.3390/jzbg3010005.

2   Jon C. Coe, 'Design and Perception: Making the Zoo Experience Real', *Zoo Biology* 4, no. 2 (1985): pp 197–208, https://doi.org/10.1002/zoo.1430040211.

3   Joyce Shettel-Neuber, 'Second- and Third-Generation Zoo Exhibits: A Comparison of Visitor, Staff, and Animal Responses', *Environment and Behavior* 20, no. 4 (1 July 1988): pp 452–73, https://doi.org/10.1177/0013916588204005; Andrew Moss, Maggie Esson and David Francis, 'Evaluation of a Third-Generation Zoo Exhibit in Relation to Visitor Behavior and Interpretation Use', *Journal of Interpretation Research* 15, no. 2 (2010): pp 11–28; Tom Smart, Gregory Counsell and Rupert J. Quinnell, 'The Impact of Immersive Exhibit Design on Visitor Behaviour and Learning at Chester Zoo, UK', *Journal of Zoo and Aquarium Research* 9, no. 3 (2021): pp 139–49, https://doi.org/10.19227/jzar.v9i3.524.

4   Gemma Edney, Tom Smart, Frederick Howat, Zoe E. Batchelor, Charlotte Hughes and Andrew Moss, 'Assessing the Effect of Interpretation Design Traits on Zoo Visitor Engagement', *Zoo Biology* 42, no. 4 (2023): pp 567–76, https://doi.org/10.1002/zoo.21759.

5   https://www.zoo.org.au/leap/connect-understand-act/.

6   Katie Major and Daniel Smith, 'Measuring the Effectiveness of Using Rangers to Deliver a Behavior Change Campaign on Sustainable Palm Oil in a UK Zoo', *Zoo Biology* 42, no. 1 (2023): pp 55–66, https://doi.org/10.1002/zoo.21697.

7   https://www.zoo.org.au/dont-palm-us-off/.

8   https://www.chesterzoo.org/news/chester-named-worlds-first-sustainable-palm-oil-city-2/.

9   https://www.waza.org/news/waza-palm-oil-scan-app/.

10   Edith MacDonald, 'Quantifying the Impact of Wellington Zoo's Persuasive Communication Campaign on Post-Visit Behavior', *Zoo Biology* 34, no. 2 (2015): pp 163–9, https://doi.org/10.1002/zoo.21197.

11   Charlotte E. Hacker and Lance J. Miller, 'Zoo Visitor Perceptions, Attitudes, and Conservation Intent after Viewing African Elephants at the San Diego Zoo Safari Park', *Zoo Biology* 35, no. 4 (2016): pp 355–61, https://doi.org/10.1002/zoo.21303; Jerry F. Luebke,

'Zoo Exhibit Experiences and Visitors' Affective Reactions:
A Preliminary Study', *Curator: The Museum Journal* 61, no. 2
(2018): pp 345–52; Lance J. Miller, Jerry F. Luebke, Jennifer
Matiasek, Douglas A. Granger, Catherine Razal, Heather J.B.
Brooks, et al, 'The Impact of In-Person and Video-Recorded
Animal Experiences on Zoo Visitors' Cognition, Affect, Empathic
Concern, and Conservation Intent', *Zoo Biology* 39, no. 6 (2020):
pp 367–73, https://doi.org/10.1002/zoo.21565.

12   Ashley Young, Kathayoon A. Khalil and Jim Wharton, 'Empathy
for Animals: A Review of the Existing Literature', *Curator:
The Museum Journal* 61, no. 2 (2018): pp 327–43, https://doi.
org/10.1111/cura.12257 discusses the different types of empathy,
and the relationships between them.

13   Edney et al, 'Assessing the Effect of Interpretation Design Traits';
Karen D. Povey and José Rios, 'Using Interpretive Animals to
Deliver Affective Messages in Zoos', *Journal of Interpretation
Research* 7, no. 2 (1 November 2002): pp 19–28, https://doi.
org/10.1177/109258720200700203.

14   Katie Roe and Andrew McConney, 'Do Zoo Visitors Come to
Learn? An Internationally Comparative, Mixed-Methods Study',
Environmental Education Research 21, no. 6 (18 August 2015):
pp 865–84, https://doi.org/10.1080/13504622.2014.940282.

15   Eric A. Jensen, Andrew Moss and Markus Gusset, 'Quantifying
Long-Term Impact of Zoo and Aquarium Visits on Biodiversity-
Related Learning Outcomes', *Zoo Biology* 36, no. 4 (2017):
pp 294–7, https://doi.org/10.1002/zoo.21372.

16   Nina Viktoria Nygren and Sanna Ojalammi, 'Conservation
Education in Zoos: A Literature Review', *TRACE ∴ Journal
for Human-Animal Studies* 4 (2018): pp 62–76, https://doi.
org/10.23984/fjhas.66540.

17   Nygren and Ojalammi, 'Conservation Education in Zoos'; Sarah
Mellish, Jillian C. Ryan, Elissa L. Pearson and Michelle R. Tuckey,
'Research Methods and Reporting Practices in Zoo and Aquarium
Conservation-Education Evaluation', *Conservation Biology* 33,
no. 1 (2019): pp 40–52, https://doi.org/10.1111/cobi.13177.

18   Courtney Collins and Ruth O'Riordan, 'Data Triangulation
Confirms Learning in the Zoo Environment', *Environmental
Education Research* 28, no. 2 (1 February 2022): pp 295–317,
https://doi.org/10.1080/13504622.2021.1974351.

19   Jamieson, 'Against Zoos', p 43.

20 Karen Hofman and Karen Hughes, 'Protecting the Great Barrier Reef: Analysing the Impact of a Conservation Documentary and Post-Viewing Strategies on Long-Term Conservation Behaviour', *Environmental Education Research* 24, no. 4 (3 April 2018): pp 521–36, https://doi.org/10.1080/13504622.2017.1303820; Jeffery C. Skibins and Ryan L. Sharp, 'Binge Watching Bears: Efficacy of Real vs. Virtual Flagship Exposure', *Journal of Ecotourism* 18, no. 2 (3 April 2019): pp 152–64, https://doi.org/10.1080/14724049.2018.1553977.

21 Marcus Carter, Sarah Webber, Simon Rawson, Wally Smith, Joseph Purdam and Emily McLeod, 'Virtual Reality in the Zoo: A Qualitative Evaluation of a Stereoscopic Virtual Reality Video Encounter with Little Penguins (*Eudyptula minor*)', *Journal of Zoo and Aquarium Research* 8, no. 4 (31 October 2020): pp 239–45, https://doi.org/10.19227/jzar.v8i4.500.

22 https://www.nottingham.ac.uk/news/twycross-zoo-hologram-project.

Chapter 6

1 Jamieson, 'Against Zoos'.

2 Marian Stamp Dawkins, *The Science of Animal Welfare: Understanding What Animals Want* (Oxford University Press, 2021).

3 Heather Browning, 'The Natural Behavior Debate: Two Conceptions of Animal Welfare', *Journal of Applied Animal Welfare Science* (27 September 2019): pp 1–13; Marian Stamp Dawkins, 'Farm Animal Welfare: Beyond "Natural" Behavior', *Science* 379, no. 6630 (27 January 2023): pp 326–8, https://doi.org/10.1126/science.ade5437.

4 Walter Veit and Heather Browning, 'Perspectival Pluralism for Animal Welfare', *European Journal for Philosophy of Science* 11, no. 9 (2021): pp 1–14.

5 Morgane Tidière, Jean-Michel Gaillard, Vérane Berger, Dennis W.H. Müller, Laurie Bingaman Lackey, Olivier Gimenez, et al, 'Comparative Analyses of Longevity and Senescence Reveal Variable Survival Benefits of Living in Zoos across Mammals', *Scientific Reports* 6, no. 1 (7 November 2016): 36361, https://doi.org/10.1038/srep36361; Marco Roller, Dennis W.H. Müller, Mads F. Bertelsen, Laurie Bingaman Lackey, Jean-Michel Hatt and Marcus Clauss, 'The Historical Development of Juvenile Mortality and Adult Longevity in Zoo-Kept Carnivores', *Zoo Biology* 40,

no. 6 (2021): pp 588–95, https://doi.org/10.1002/zoo.21639; Lara Scherer, Laurie Bingaman Lackey, Marcus Clauss, Katrin Gries, David Hagan, Arne Lawrenz, et al, 'The Historical Development of Zoo Elephant Survivorship', *Zoo Biology* 42, no. 2 (2023): pp 328–38, https://doi.org/10.1002/zoo.21733; Morgane Tidière, Fernando Colchero, Johanna Staerk, Michael J. Adkesson, Ditte H. Andersen, Lucie Bland, et al, 'Survival Improvements of Marine Mammals in Zoological Institutions Mirror Historical Advances in Human Longevity', *Proceedings of the Royal Society B: Biological Sciences* 290, no. 2009 (18 October 2023): 20231895, https://doi.org/10.1098/rspb.2023.1895.

6   Eileen K. Tuite, Simon A. Moss, Clive J. Phillips and Samantha J. Ward, 'Why Are Enrichment Practices in Zoos Difficult to Implement Effectively?', *Animals* 12, no. 5 (23 February 2022): 554, https://doi.org/10.3390/ani12050554.

7   Marina Salas, Daan W. Laméris, Arno Depoortere, Lise Plessers and Jonas Verspeek, 'Zoo Visitor Attitudes Are More Influenced by Animal Behaviour than Environmental Enrichment Appearance', *Animals* 11, no. 7 (July 2021): 1971, https://doi.org/10.3390/ani11071971.

8   Justine Cole and David Fraser, 'Zoo Animal Welfare: The Human Dimension', *Journal of Applied Animal Welfare Science* 21, no. sup1 (31 August 2018): pp 49–58, https://doi.org/10.1080/10888705.2018.1513839; Geoff Hosey and Vicky Melfi, 'Human–Animal Bonds Between Zoo Professionals and the Animals in Their Care', *Zoo Biology* 31, no. 1 (2012): pp 13–26, https://doi.org/10.1002/zoo.20359; Sabrina Brando, Chris Dold, Vinícius Donisete Lima Rodrigues Goulart and Todd Robeck, 'Factors Influencing the Development of Human–Animal Relationships at SeaWorld Entertainment Parks', *Aquatic Mammals* 49, no. 3 (15 May 2023): pp 294–307, https://doi.org/10.1578/AM.49.3.2023.294.

9   https://www.waza.org/priorities/animal-welfare/2023-animal-welfare-goal/.

10 David J. Mellor, Ngaio J. Beausoleil, Katherine E. Littlewood, Andrew N. McLean, Paul D. McGreevy, Bidda Jones, et al, 'The 2020 Five Domains Model: Including Human–Animal Interactions in Assessments of Animal Welfare', *Animals* 10, no. 10 (2020): 1870.

11 Jessica C. Whitham and Nadja Wielebnowski, 'Animal-Based Welfare Monitoring: Using Keeper Ratings as an Assessment Tool', *Zoo Biology* 28, no. 6 (2009): pp 545–60, https://doi.org/10.1002/zoo.20281.

12   See review in Narelle Jones, Sally L. Sherwen, Rachel Robbins, David J. McLelland and Alexandra L. Whittaker, 'Welfare Assessment Tools in Zoos: From Theory to Practice', *Veterinary Sciences* 9, no. 4 (1 April 2022): 170, https://doi.org/10.3390/vetsci9040170.

13   If one takes an interest-based account of rights, such as that advocated by philosopher Alasdair Cochrane: Alasdair Cochrane, *Animal Rights Without Liberation: Applied Ethics and Human Obligations* (Columbia University Press, 2012).

14   Hannah M. Buchanan-Smith and Inbal Badihi, 'The Psychology of Control: Effects of Control over Supplementary Light on Welfare of Marmosets', *Applied Animal Behaviour Science* 137, no. 3 (1 March 2012): pp 166–74, https://doi.org/10.1016/j.applanim.2011.07.002.

15   I.R. Inglis, Bjorn Forkman and John Lazarus, 'Free Food or Earned Food? A Review and Fuzzy Model of Contrafreeloading', *Animal Behaviour* 53, no. 6 (1 June 1997): pp 1171–91, https://doi.org/10.1006/anbe.1996.0320.

16   Lauren A. Leotti, Sheena S. Iyengar, and Kevin N. Ochsner, 'Born to Choose', *Trends in Cognitive Sciences* 14, no. 10 (October 2010): pp 457–63, https://doi.org/10.1016/j.tics.2010.08.001.

17   Laura M. Kurtycz, Katherine E. Wagner and Stephen R. Ross, 'The Choice to Access Outdoor Areas Affects the Behavior of Great Apes', *Journal of Applied Animal Welfare Science* 17, no. 3 (3 July 2014): pp 185–97, https://doi.org/10.1080/10888705.2014.896213.

18   See range of options discussed in Stephanie M. Allard and Meredith J. Bashaw, 'Empowering Zoo Animals', in *Scientific Foundations of Zoos and Aquariums*, ed Allison B. Kaufman, Meredith J. Bashaw and Terry L. Maple, 1st edn (Cambridge University Press, 2019), pp 241–73, https://doi.org/10.1017/9781108183147.010; and Jon Coe and Julia Hoy, 'Choice, Control and Computers: Empowering Wildlife in Human Care', *Multimodal Technologies and Interaction* 4, no. 4 (14 December 2020): 92, https://doi.org/10.3390/mti4040092.

19   Coe and Hoy, 'Choice, Control and Computers'.

20   Roosa Piitulainen and Ilyena Hirskyj-Douglas, 'Music for Monkeys: Building Methods to Design with White-Faced Sakis for Animal-Driven Audio Enrichment Devices', *Animals* 10, no. 10 (October 2020): 1768, https://doi.org/10.3390/ani10101768; Jordyn Truax and Jennifer Vonk, 'Silence Is Golden: Auditory Preferences in Zoo-Housed Gorillas', *Journal of Applied Animal*

Welfare Science 26, no. 3 (3 July 2023): pp 404–19, https://doi.org/10.1080/10888705.2021.1968400.

21   Marcus Carter, Sally Sherwen and Sarah Webber, 'An Evaluation of Interactive Projections as Digital Enrichment for Orangutans', *Zoo Biology* 40, no. 2 (2021): pp 107–14, https://doi.org/10.1002/zoo.21587.

22   Jake S. Veasey, 'In Pursuit of Peak Animal Welfare; the Need to Prioritize the Meaningful over the Measurable', *Zoo Biology* 36, no. 6 (2017): pp 413–25, https://doi.org/10.1002/zoo.21390.

23   Lori Gruen and Erika Fleury, 'Animal Welfare, Animal Rights, and a Sanctuary Ethos', in *Nonhuman Primate Welfare: From History, Science, and Ethics to Practice*, ed Lauren M. Robinson and Alexander Weiss (Springer International Publishing, 2023), pp 627–41, https://doi.org/10.1007/978-3-030-82708-3_26.

24   Jamieson, 'Zoos Revisited', pp 63–4.

Chapter 7

1   Ros Clubb and Georgia Mason, 'Natural Behavioural Biology as a Risk Factor in Carnivore Welfare: How Analysing Species Differences Could Help Zoos Improve Enclosures', *Applied Animal Behaviour Science* 102, no. 3–4 (February 2007): pp 303–28; Georgia J. Mason, 'Species Differences in Responses to Captivity: Stress, Welfare and the Comparative Method', *Trends in Ecology & Evolution* 25, no. 12 (1 December 2010): pp 713–21, https://doi.org/10.1016/j.tree.2010.08.011; Emma L. Mellor, Heather K. McDonald Kinkaid, Michael T. Mendl, Innes C. Cuthill, Yvonne R.A. van Zeeland and Georgia J. Mason, 'Nature Calls: Intelligence and Natural Foraging Style Predict Poor Welfare in Captive Parrots', *Proceedings of the Royal Society B: Biological Sciences* 288, no. 1960 (13 October 2021): 20211952, https://doi.org/10.1098/rspb.2021.1952.

2   Andrew Mooney, Dalia A. Conde, Kevin Healy and Yvonne M. Buckley, 'A System Wide Approach to Managing Zoo Collections for Visitor Attendance and in situ Conservation', *Nature Communications* 11, no. 1 (4 February 2020): 584, https://doi.org/10.1038/s41467-020-14303-2.

3   https://www.theguardian.com/us-news/2022/may/19/the-person-in-the-room-court-mulls-if-elephant-has-human-rights.

4   Terry L. Maple, 'Strategic Collection Planning and Individual Animal Welfare', *Journal of the American Veterinary Medical*

Association 223, no. 7 (1 October 2003): pp 966–9, https://doi.
org/10.2460/javma.2003.223.966.

5   Heather Browning, 'No Room at the Zoo: Management
Euthanasia and Animal Welfare', *Journal of Agricultural and
Environmental Ethics* 31, no. 4 (August 2018): pp 483–98,
https://doi.org/10.1007/s10806-018-9741-8.

6   H. Barnes, 'How Many Healthy Animals do Zoos Put Down?',
BBC News, 2014, http://www.bbc.com/news/magazine-26356099.

7   See Josh Milburn, *Just Fodder: The Ethics of Feeding Animals*
(McGill-Queen's University Press, 2022) for in-depth discussion of
the use of animals as feed.

8   Matilda Gibbons, Andrew Crump, Meghan Barrett, Sajedeh
Sarlak, Jonathan Birch and Lars Chittka, 'Can Insects Feel Pain?
A Review of the Neural and Behavioural Evidence', *Advances in
Insect Physiology* 63 (2022): pp 155–229, https://doi.org/10.1016/
bs.aiip.2022.10.001.

9   Milburn, *Just Fodder*.

10   Heather Bacon, Catriona Bell, Cathy M. Dwyer, Natalie Waran,
Yan Qing, Liu Xia, et al, 'Exploration of Cultural Norms and
Behavioural Beliefs about Zoo Animal Behaviour, Welfare, Ethics
and Husbandry Practices in a Sample of the International Zoo
Community', *Zoo Biology* 42, no. 3 (2023): pp 416–28, https://doi.
org/10.1002/zoo.21749.

FURTHER READING

Stephen St C. Bostock, *Zoos and Animal Rights: The Ethics of Keeping Animals* (Routledge, 1993).

Sabrina Brando and Hannah M. Buchanan-Smith, 'The 24/7 Approach to Promoting Optimal Welfare for Captive Wild Animals', *Behavioural Processes* (2018) 156: 83–95.

Heather Browning and Walter Veit, 'Freedom and Animal Welfare', *Animals* (2021) 11(4): 1148. https://doi.org/10.3390/ani11041148

Jeremy Cherfas, *Zoo 2000: A Look Beyond the Bars* (BBC Publications, 1984).

Eduardo J. Fernandez, James E. Brereton and Jon Coe, 'How Do We Plan for the Zoo Exhibit of the Future?', *Applied Animal Behaviour Science* (2023), 106085. https://doi.org/10.1016/j.applanim.2023.106085

Jenny Gray, *Zoo Ethics: The Challenges of Compassionate Conservation* (Cornell University Press, 2017).

Lori Gruen (ed), *The Ethics of Captivity* (Oxford University Press, 2014).

Heini Hediger, *Man and Animal in the Zoo* (Delacorte Press, 1969).

Geoff Hosey, Vicky Melfi and Sheila Pankhurst, *Zoo Animals: Behaviour, Management, and Welfare* (Oxford University Press, 2013).

Michael Hutchins, Brandie Smith and Ruth Allard, 'In Defense of Zoos and Aquariums: The Ethical Basis for Keeping Wild Animals in Captivity', *Journal of the American Veterinary Medical Association* (2003) 223(7): 958–66.

Allison B. Kaufman, Meredith J. Bashaw and Terry L. Maple (eds), *Scientific Foundations of Zoos and Aquariums* (Cambridge University Press, 2019).

Vernon N. Kisling (ed), *Zoo and Aquarium History: Ancient Animal Collections to Zoological Gardens* (CRC Press, 2001).

Randy Malamud, *Reading Zoos: Representations of Animals and Captivity* (New York University Press, 1998).

Terry L. Maple and Bonnie M. Perdue, *Zoo Animal Welfare* (Springer, 2013).

Nicole Mazur, *After the Ark?* (Melbourne University Publishing, 1997).

Ben A. Minteer, Jane Maienschein and James P. Collins (eds), *The Ark and Beyond: The Evolution of Zoo and Aquarium Conservation* (University of Chicago Press, 2018).

Bob Mullan and Garry Marvin, *Zoo Culture* (MW Books Ltd, 1987).

Bryan G. Norton, Michael Hutchins, Elizabeth F. Stevens and Terry L. Maple (eds), *Ethics on the Ark* (Washington and London: Smithsonian Institution Press, 1995).

George B. Rabb, 'The Changing Roles of Zoological Parks in Conserving Biological Diversity', *American Zoologist* (1994) 34(1): 159–64. https://doi.org/10.1093/icb/34.1.159

Paul A. Rees, *An Introduction to Zoo Biology and Management* (John Wiley & Sons, 2011).

Paul Rose (ed), *The Behavioural Biology of Zoo Animals* (CRC Press, 2022).

Paul E. Rose and Lisa M. Riley, 'Expanding the Role of the Future Zoo: Wellbeing Should Become the Fifth Aim for Modern Zoos', *Frontiers in Psychology* (2022) 13: 1018722. https://doi.org/10.3389/fpsyg.2022.1018722

World Association of Zoos and Aquariums, *Caring for Wildlife: The World Zoo and Aquarium Animal Welfare Strategy* (2015). https://www.waza.org/

World Association of Zoos and Aquariums, *Committing to Conservation: The World Zoo and Aquarium Conservation Strategy* (2015). https://www.waza.org/

INDEX

References to figures are in *italics* and to tables are in **bold**.